W9-BYA-592

Saint
Training

ZONDERKIDZ

Saint Training
Copyright © 2010 by Elizabeth Fixmer

This title is also available as a Zondervan ebook.
Visit www.zondervan.com/ebooks.

Requests for information should be addressed to:

Zonderkidz, *Grand Rapids, Michigan* 49530

Library of Congress Cataloging-in-Publication Data

Fixmer, Elizabeth, 1952 –
    Saint training / Elizabeth Fixmer.
        p.   cm.
        Summary: During the turbulent 1960s, sixth-grader Mary Clare makes a deal
    with God: she will try to become a saint if He provides for her large, cash-
    strapped family.
        ISBN 978-0-310-72018-8 (hardcover)
        [1. Catholics – Fiction. 2. Christian life – Fiction. 3. Conduct of life – Fiction.
    4. Family problems – Fiction. 5. Schools – Fiction. 6. Nineteen sixties – Fiction.]
    I. Title.
    PZ7.F5927Sai 2010
    [Fic]–dc22   2010010831

Editor: Kathleen Kerr
Art direction: Cindy Davis
Cover design: Sarah Molegraaf
Interior design and composition: Carlos Eluterio Estrada and Tina Henderson

Printed in the United States of America

10 11 12 13 14 15 /DCI/ 22 21 20 19 18 17 16 15 14 13 12 11 10 9 8 7 6 5 4 3 2 1

Saint Training

Elizabeth Fixmer

ZONDER**kidz**

ZONDERVAN.com/
AUTHOR**TRACKER**
follow your favorite authors

To my mother, Audrey Mettel Fixmer, who has always been my source of courage, strength, and inspiration. And to my niece, Hillary, who introduced me to middle grade and young adult novels, insisting that I read every book she read so we could talk about them.

Part 1
Spring 1967

Mary Clare O'Brian
188 Jackson Street
Littleburg, Wisconsin 53538

Saint Mary Magdalene Convent
1123 Good Shepherd Road
Minneapolis, Minnesota 55199

March 25, 1967

Dear Reverend Mother,

My name is Mary Clare O'Brian. I am in sixth grade and I am writing because I want to become a Good Shepherd nun. I like the Good Shepherd nuns best because you work with unwed mothers and their babies. I love little babies.

I have lots of experience with kids. God gives my family a new baby every year even though we have more than we can handle now. Everyone says that I am very mature for my age because of how well I take care of my little brothers and sisters. Also I'm a good leader. The nuns at school can be really strict and when I'm in charge of the little kids at home, I have to be strict lots of times.

I saw *The Sound of Music* where the Mother Superior helped Julie Andrews face her problems. I could do that. Everybody tells me their problems, and I'm good at solutions.

Another reason I'm interested in being a Good Shepherd nun is because of the habits you wear. I love them. Most nuns wear all black except for the wimple and cowl, but that's like going to a funeral every day, don't you think? I love the white and cream of your habits along with the light brown. I like the veil too. It all goes together well and looks sophisticated. I think the habit will make my brown eyes look bigger. My hair is also brown, but that won't show. Just between you and me. I'll be glad to cover up my curly hair because it's impossible. Right now, I just offer it up to God.

One problem I have is this: Sister Charlotte, my teacher, says I'd never make it in the convent unless I was the Mother Superior. I think she has a good point. As I already mentioned, I'm a leader, not a follower, which is why I have trouble with obedience.

I am president of my sixth grade class. This year I wrote and directed a play my class put on for the whole school. I also played the lead role. I used to be president of my Camp Fire Girls troop, but this year I ran for vice president to give someone else a turn. I get good grades, mostly A's. I always get A's in Religion and usually in Conduct if I get along with the teacher.

Reverend Mother, I think I should be a Mother Superior because I'm the kind of person that everyone tells their problems to. Even my own mother confides in me. She says I make her feel better.

I would like to join the convent right after eighth grade before I start liking boys too much. I'm already having problems with boys liking me. Gregory, in my class, throws spitballs at me and told my best friend that he likes me. I haven't told him that I want to be God's bride yet. Do you think I should?

Could you please write back and tell me more about your convent and how to become the Mother Superior? Do you get chosen by the Pope, or get a sign from God, or do you hold an election? If you're chosen through voting I know a lot about campaigning because my father campaigned for President Johnson. I could make signs and stuff.

Please let me know as soon as possible.

I can't wait to hear from you!

Sincerely,
Mary Clare O'Brian

1

Mary Clare finished her Social Studies test and turned it upside down to wait for the rest of the class. It was easy, mostly essay, and on a subject that Mary Clare had heard a lot about at home around the dinner table: civil rights. She couldn't believe that Negroes had to sit on the back of the bus in the South and even drink from different water fountains. They were fighting for basic rights, especially the right to vote. Mary Clare liked to imagine that a Negro girl entered her very class at Saint Maria Goretti School. She would show her around, become her friend, even hold the drinking fountain on for her.

Now her face scrunched into a yawn she fought to control. She was tired from being up almost all night—first listening to her parents fight, then praying for the perfect plan to make things better for her family. After she came up with the perfect plan, she couldn't sleep at all.

She was going to become a saint. She had written to Mother Superior because she figured that becoming the Mother Superior of a convent was the best way to climb the ladder toward sainthood. Saint Theresa, the Little Flower, was a nun before she became a saint, and so was Saint Claire. Mary Clare didn't want to tell Mother Superior that she wanted to become a saint, of course, because that would make her seem conceited. Becoming a saint would be her own secret—a secret she shared with God alone.

She could see herself now—all dressed in white and a shiny gold halo crowning her head. Her body shining like the Virgin Mary statue Sister Charlotte gave her when she got an A in Conduct. If you held the little statue under a light for a few minutes you could take it into the darkest of closets and it *glowed*.

Mary Clare opened her eyes when she heard whispering in front of the classroom. Sister Charlotte nodded to Kelly from behind her desk, and Kelly left the room, her long blonde braids trailing behind her. When Mary Clare looked down at her desk, she saw that Kelly had dropped a note on her desk on her way to ask to be excused. *Chocolate Coke after school? My treat.*

She turned the note over and responded. *I'm supposed to walk my little sisters home, but what the heck, I'd much rather have a chocolate Coke with you. So—yes!* She could slip it to Kelly when she came back from the bathroom. She folded the note and waited for Kelly to return.

But sending a note in class was a sin, she realized. Mary Clare sat back hard in her seat, contemplating how difficult this whole saint thing was going to be. If she was going to become a saint, she shouldn't send notes in class or disobey her mother by going to the Counter after school, even if they were little venial sins and not a big deal. She would confess them on Saturday, of course.

She thought about the two sins. They were both venial but disobedience had to be a bigger sin than passing a note. She wondered why the Catholic Church hadn't thought of this—making more gradations of venial sins. Well, she'd hold onto that idea, maybe create a venial one category and venial two and three categories as well. She'd wait till she was Mother Superior, first.

Mary Clare lifted her desktop and slipped the note inside one of the books she had gotten that morning from the St. Maria Goretti School library: *Saint Therese Martin*, along with *St. Joan: The Girl Soldier, Bernadette and the Lady*, and the most important book of all, *The Baltimore Catechism*. That book taught everything anybody needed to know about becoming a good Catholic. Heck, studying *The Baltimore Catechism* alone would give her all she needed to become a saint.

She wondered whether or not she should be using the word "heck."

When Kelly returned, Mary Clare smiled and nodded as she walked by the desk. Technically a smile and nod was not even a venial sin, she figured. It was neither "talking in class" nor "passing notes," both of which counted. All right, she'd just commit the one — category two — venial sin: disobedience. She wanted a chance to tell Kelly about her mom's pregnancy and her idea about Matthew's band. If that was the only one she committed today, it would be okay. Sister Charlotte said even saints committed some sins. She'd reassure her sisters that they'd be just fine and tell them to look both ways before they crossed the streets, and then she'd go to the Counter for a chocolate Coke. But, after that, she'd really have to start working on becoming a saint.

Her thoughts returned to her parents last night. She'd been sound asleep when she heard her father yell "No!" and her mother burst into tears. Her own head was throbbing from the soup cans she had wound tightly around her hair. (They were supposed to take away the curls.) She'd pulled the tightest one out and rubbed her head where the throbbing was. She couldn't catch everything they were saying. Her mom kept crying, loud belly sobs, and she could hear her dad stomping around and around the bedroom, the way he did when he was upset. "We can't afford another baby," he'd said.

Mary Clare had plugged her ears before she heard anything more. But she did hear Johnny whining across the room. He was standing in his crib, his chubby little arms outstretched toward her. She hurried to pick him up and laid him down in her single bed, praying he'd go right back to sleep. Then she scooched over to make room for Martha, who stood by the bed clinging to her white bear and looking terrified. That was the thing about sharing a bedroom with two of the little kids: if they were afraid because of a storm or a fight, or woke up feeling sick, they usually turned to her for comfort—especially when Dad was home. Neither parent liked to be awakened in the middle of the night. Mary Clare didn't usually mind, except when somebody threw up in her bed, like Martha that time. But last night, when Margaret and Gabriella came rushing in from their bedroom, there was no way Mary Clare could fit all of them in her bed, so she ushered the whole brood back to the room Anne, Gabriella, and Margaret shared, and they cuddled together in the girls' double bed.

"Let's say our prayers," Mary Clare suggested. She waited until the kids stopped wiggling around trying to get comfortable, and then they recited their nighttime prayer in whispers. "Now I lay me down to sleep. I pray the Lord my soul to keep. If I should die before I wake, I pray the Lord my soul to take." Then began the litany of family members from oldest to youngest: "God bless Mommy, Daddy, Matthew, Mark, Luke, Mary Clare, Anne, Gabriella, Margaret, Martha, and Johnny." In an almost inaudible whisper Gabriella added, "And God bless the baby in Mommy's tummy."

After a moment of silence Martha poked Mary Clare on the shoulder. "Tell us a story," she begged.

"Yeah," Gabriella said, "but not about saints or anything religious."

Johnny cuddled up with his head on her shoulder, his thumb and torn blankie in his mouth.

Mary Clare used her most soothing voice. "Once upon a time a little prince and four beautiful princesses lived together in a tall castle with everything they could imagine wanting. They were very happy ..."

Johnny's lashes stopped fluttering almost immediately, and Mary Clare watched the rhythmic rise and fall of Martha's chest just minutes later. Gabriella yawned. "And there were tiny fairies in the courtyard," Mary Clare added. But a minute more and they were all asleep—all except Mary Clare, who couldn't be comforted by a fairy tale. She lay wide awake.

She hated this: money problems, too many kids, another baby on the way. *That's why Mom doesn't sing anymore when we do dishes and laundry,* Mary Clare thought. She missed the mother who laughed with her friends over coffee, who made fancy appetizers for cocktail parties, who sewed blue eyelet curtains for her room. She wished Matthew would come home from the Seminary so she would have someone to talk to about all this.

Lord, help my family. Please, please give us enough money so Mom and Dad can be happy again.

She stopped. She was sick of this prayer. Why wasn't God answering? He used to answer her prayers all the time.

But that was before. She was little then. She could say "Please God, we need money for my brother's birthday," and God would send it. She would just find it—on the sidewalk, down by the river, in a pile of leaves. Five, ten, even twenty dollar bills. She even prayed the family into a new car when she was only four. It was right before the family moved from Minnesota to Wisconsin because her father stopped teaching and started his job selling textbooks to schools. She prayed fervently every night, and one night while she was sleeping God put a brand-new 1958 Ford in the driveway. That was when Mary Clare knew it was her job to pray for stuff. Even when she learned that the car came from the job Dad had just started, she knew it was really from God. She had prayed that car into the driveway—even her brothers thought so.

Then it just stopped ... when ... when she was about seven. Mary Clare's eyes opened wide and she sat up in bed carefully so none of the kids woke up. Seven—seven was when sins started to count. That was when God stopped listening to her prayers.

When Mary Clare got up two soup cans rolled out of her hair. Now she knew the problem: God would only listen to her if her soul was pure. If she was going to make her mother happy again, she would have to be a saint right away.

She made a plan. She would study, she would practice saint-like behavior, and she would become a nun. Many of the girl saints had been nuns before being sainted, so she figured becoming a nun was the perfect stepping stone to her real goal. She'd be so darned good she wouldn't have a thing to confess on Saturdays.

Mary Clare explained the deal to God. *If you take care of my family—give them enough money, make my parents happy ... I'll become a saint.* She repeated it several times in case it was hard for God to hear through all of her sins. By the time she'd gotten to sleep, it was almost time to get up.

Now Mary Clare was so tired she could hardly keep her eyes open. She covered her mouth to suppress a yawn just as Sister Charlotte, who sat at her desk in the front of the classroom, looked at the clock.

"My goodness!" Sister Charlotte said, standing up. "You all must have finished your tests ages ago! Pass them to the front." She clapped her hands together twice and smiled her movie star smile. The dimples that only showed when she smiled melted into her cheeks. Mary Clare thought she was the most cheerful nun she'd ever met.

Tommy Johnson sat in the desk behind Mary Clare. Instead of passing the papers forward he poked the back of her neck with his pencil. He was obnoxious like that. She turned to take the papers and glared at his freckled face, but immediately wished she hadn't. Saint Theresa wouldn't have given Tommy a dirty look. She would have smiled and offered Tommy's poke up to Jesus. Mary Clare was momentarily flooded with disappointment in herself, but the feeling quickly shifted to irritation at Tommy. Tommy was just the kind of bratty boy who could keep her from becoming a saint. She contemplated how Saint Theresa held onto her loving manner, even when people were mean to her, and sighed. Saint Theresa was so much like the Virgin Mary—obedient, quiet, sweet, and kind. Almost the opposite of Mary Clare. She was going to have to work hard to become a saint.

Sister collected the quizzes from each row. Students automatically started pulling open the tops of their desks to retrieve their English books for the last class of the day, but Sister held up her hand.

"No, class. No English today. I have a surprise for you instead. This year, for the first time ever, the sixth grade will be entering a diocesan essay contest," Sister Charlotte announced, "and I'm excited for you all. The topic is 'What a Religious Vocation Means to Me' and ..." Tommy groaned behind Mary Clare and Jen Fitzgerald stuck her index finger in her mouth like she was going to throw up. Several snickers followed.

"And ... wait a minute. This contest has cash prizes! The diocese has never had prizes before, but this year an elderly couple from Madison made a donation specifically to help children start thinking about vocations as nuns or priests."

Mary Clare raised her hand so high she was completely out of her seat. "How much are the prizes?"

Sister's nose scrunched the way it did when she smiled. "The third prize is fifteen dollars."

Oohs and aahs plus one whistle.

"Second prize is double that."

"Thirty bucks!" Ron Lyons announced. "A kid could get a Schwinn for that!"

"Or Kelly could get two Barbie dolls with a whole bunch of clothes for her and Mary Clare." It was Tommy, of course.

"You don't care about the first prize?" Sister asked, feigning shock.

"Yes!" everyone said in unison.

"Fifty dollars, but"—Sister stopped while everyone took in noisy breaths—"you have steep competition. Remember, it's every sixth grade class in the whole diocese."

Mary Clare couldn't breathe. She pictured the diocesan directory. It was way bigger than the Littleburg, Wisconsin phone book. There had to be fifty different churches in it. She looked around. There were forty-three kids in her class. She didn't even want to think of how many essays that would be.

It didn't matter. She had to win. Fifty dollars! Mary Clare's parents would be so relieved. Her mom might even be okay with having another baby. *Let me win first prize, Lord, and I'll know you've accepted my deal to be become a saint.* She would start being good now. Forget the chocolate Coke with Kelly; she'd obediently walk the kids home. *Please, God. Please.*

"Don't look so glum, kids. You have the same chance of winning as everyone else. So let's take the focus off the prizes and think about the essay itself. You will also be getting an English grade for your essay, so make it sparkle! You won't get class time to write it but the contest deadline isn't until Monday, May 1, so they'll be due on Friday, April 28. That's a little over two weeks. Ask God to help you do your best work."

The squeal of the intercom made everyone cover their ears. Mary Clare looked at the clock. In three minutes the bell would ring. Sister Agnes always managed to time the afternoon messages so that the bell rang the minute she was done speaking. There was some speculation among the students that she actually rehearsed the announcements with her stopwatch.

"May I have your attention, please? Saint Maria Goretti School will begin selling World's Finest Chocolate Bars starting Monday. Each child is expected to sell a minimum of twenty chocolate bars to help pay for school supplies. So tell your parents and start thinking of people who will want to enjoy these delicious chocolate treats. Next week begins our annual campaign to collect money for pagan babies. Remember that saving a pagan baby is saving a soul. The boy or girl from each class who contributes the most money will be given a scapular blessed by the late Pope John XXIII. Remember that by wearing a scapular every day, you are protected at the time of death. So take your allowance or offer to do extra chores around the house to collect money for this worthy cause. A reminder that all children are expected to attend daily Mass. I have been advised that a few of you are congregating outside Sentry Foods instead of attending. In the future, anyone missing Mass will receive detention and parents will be notified. Also, the sixth grade Camp Fire Girls will have a bake sale on Monday after school. Finally, will Mary Clare O'Brian please report to the office."

"Mary Clare's in trou-ble," Tommy said. A few kids snickered but stopped when Gregory chimed in.

"Well, I'm sure she's not going to get spanked by Father Dwyer for breaking a window, like some people I know." Now everybody laughed except Tommy, whose face matched his red hair. He was the first kid out of the room.

Mary Clare's heart sank. The only time she ever got called to the office was because of money. At least she wouldn't have to let Kelly know that she couldn't go out for the chocolate Coke. She shrugged at Kelly. What could she do? Nice of God to take away the temptation.

As all the other kids rushed out of the classroom, heading to their lockers to exchange books or clamoring down the two flights of stairs to the main entrance, Mary Clare walked slowly in the opposite direction. She dreaded going to the office of Sister Agnes, or, as the students called her behind her back, "Sister Agony." When she was halfway down the long, dimly lit corridor she could make out the image of Sister Agony sitting behind her desk in her office at the end of the hall. *Lord,* she prayed, *please help me be sweet like Mary. Please help me not show Sister how much I can't stand her.*

2

Sister Agnes was the shortest adult Mary Clare knew. At eleven, Mary Clare already towered over the nun. Sister Agnes was looking up into her face, the wimple on her neck stretched so far you couldn't see the pleats. It looked like it was about to choke her.

"Sit," she said, pointing to a chair.

"Yes, Sister." Mary Clare sat. Sister remained standing. She reached into a basket on top of the dark wooden desk that was so large it took up most of the office. Behind it, a picture of the Sacred Heart of Jesus and another of the Virgin Mary looked sorrowfully down at Mary Clare. A corner window overlooked St. Maria Goretti Church and the front of the school where 350 kids were scampering, their uniforms a blur of black, white, and red.

When Sister Agnes found the envelope she was looking for, she held it out to Mary Clare. But suddenly reconsidering, she jerked the envelope back, opened the flap, and licked it so it was securely sealed.

"Give this to your parents—and don't open it. It's none of your business." She pursed her lips for emphasis. Stamped in bold red letters on the outside of the envelope were the words

FINAL NOTICE! The names of her parents, Paul and Grace O'Brian, were centered in neat cursive.

Mary Clare could feel the heat rising in her face. She managed to keep a straight face, reminding herself that if she were going to become a saint, she must offer this humiliation up to Jesus.

"You have to understand that I have a school to run, Mary Clare. I have bills to pay. Good Catholics pay their bills on time. I'm tired of having to get after your parents for tuition, books— and now this. If your parents don't want to see Gabriella be the only one in her First Communion class to walk down the aisle without a missal and rosary ..."

Mary Clare stood. She turned on her heel and crammed the envelope in her uniform jacket. "Good-night, Sister." She knew her eyes were as cold as her voice in spite of her efforts to the contrary.

"Good-night," Sister said. Her voice held no mercy.

Mary Clare made her way through the long empty hallway and down the two flights of stairs to the antiseptic smell of Mr. Gordon's bucket. He was already mopping the entrance.

"Careful not to slip," he said. "I don't want to see you get hurt."

Mary Clare only nodded, too angry to make polite conversation, even with Mr. Gordon. She expected the girls to be on the front steps, but instead it was Gregory leaning against the wall. Mary Clare looked past him to search out her sisters.

"They're playing on the merry-go-round," Gregory said. He pointed to the side playground. "I just wanted to make sure you were all right."

"I'm fine," Mary Clare lied.

"So are you planning to win the diocesan essay contest?"

"Yup," Mary Clare said.

Gregory laughed. "You're so conceited." He folded his arms in front of himself and raised one eyebrow. "You know, I just might be the big winner."

"I doubt it," Mary Clare said. It felt good to get back into the regular banter she and Gregory shared.

"We're over here," Anne hollered. She was the only one of the kids with blonde hair. Everyone else had varying shades of brown.

Mary Clare backed up toward Anne, saying her final words to Gregory. "You'd better start writing. It'll take lots of revisions if you want second place."

●

Mary Clare could hear squeals of laughter from Margaret and Gabriella as she turned onto the side playground. Anne, the third grader, was pushing Gabriella and Margaret—second and first grade—making the wheel go faster and faster. The little girls were holding on and giggling. Mary Clare took over for a few minutes to give Anne a turn to enjoy the ride before they started on the mile walk home.

"How come you got called to the office, Mary Clare?" Anne asked. Her blonde pigtails bobbed as she walked.

Mary Clare shrugged. She didn't have to answer because Margaret was pulling on her blazer sleeve to get her attention.

"Lookit! Lookit!" Margaret held out her hand to show Mary Clare the four pennies she was holding. Her bright smiled showed a mouth minus two upper teeth and two lower, right in front. "Can we stop at the pharmacy to get Pixy Stix? I can get one for all of us!" Margaret puffed up her chest proudly.

Gabriella skipped backwards ahead of them, her chocolate eyes wide with excitement. "I want cherry," she said. Her white blouse had a large red stain on it . . . probably from the raspberry Jell-O they'd had at lunch.

"I want grape," Anne said.

Mary Clare slowed down to consider the idea. They weren't near a crosswalk and the pharmacy was coming up on the opposite side of the street. "Okay, but we'd better be careful and hold hands."

Mary Clare led them across the busy street past Sentry Foods and into the pharmacy, where the usual swells of school kids had dwindled to a few seventh and eighth graders sharing french fries and Cokes at the counter. When each girl had picked out her Pixy Stix and Margaret held out her pennies, she let out a squeal. "There's only three pennies!" she cried. Mary Clare helped the girls look on the tiled floor and on the sidewalk outside, but the penny was gone.

Mary Clare knelt next to Margaret and wiped her tears on the hankie she had taken to sticking up her sleeve like the nuns did. "It's okay, Margaret. I put mine back already."

"But I wanted to treat you," Margaret sobbed.

Mary Clare hugged her little sister close. It really was okay. Margaret's gesture took away some of the sting from her encounter with Sister Agony. Mary Clare ushered the girls out of the store and back across the street to resume their walk home. Home was eight more blocks, but Mary Clare counted it as eleven because the two blocks on Jackson Street were so long. She divided the walk into three sections in her mind. The first three blocks on Madison Avenue constituted the commercial section of the walk. They passed the Clark station and the Frosty Freeze where two men were optimistically washing the windows—a sign that they were getting ready to open after the long winter. That brought them to the second section; four blocks of Victorian houses, some of them huge, interspersed with a few smaller modern houses. Jackson Street was the third and hard-est section. It consisted of two very long blocks up a steep hill. Their home was at the top, the outer edge of town. It overlooked acres and acres of cornfields. By the time they reached Jackson Mary Clare could count on complaints from the younger girls, and today was no exception.

"Margie Cook gets a ride home every day," Margaret said.

"She lives in the country," Anne said.

Margaret turned toward Mary Clare. "I want to live on a farm with horses and cows and pigs."

Mary Clare stopped when she saw that Margaret's face and blouse were smeared with the powdery purple from the Pixy Stix. "You *guys*," she complained, looking at Margaret and Gabriella's blouses. "We've got to get you changed before Mom sees you, and I'll have to try to get those stains out. That's *all* Mom needs."

The girls looked stricken. They followed a little way behind Mary Clare in silence, which hurt Mary Clare far more than her outburst was worth. The last thing she wanted was to make them worry about Mom.

God, please help me to be more patient with the kids.

Mary Clare turned to face her sisters who were marching in perfect step in a straight line, oldest to youngest, behind her. Mary Clare had to laugh. She stood tall like a commander. "Okay, troops, are you ready to go to war?" Margaret and Anne marched forward proudly, but Gabriella immediately stepped out of formation and raised one fist in the air. "Hell no, we won't go!" she shouted. She backed up and looked surprised at the shock on her sisters' faces. "Well, that's what Matthew and his seminary friends say all the time," she argued.

"You know better than to say that word. When those guys say it it's to protest the war in Vietnam." Mary Clare wasn't sure protesting made it okay to say "hell" either.

Gabriella twirled around defiantly and pretended to hold a sign in the air. "All we are saay-ing is give peace a chance." The other girls joined in, singing it loud and proud right in front of the Turner's white-pillared house. They were Southerners and some kind of Protestant. Becky was the same age as Mary Clare so they played together sometimes, but Mrs. Turner always seemed to regard Mary Clare suspiciously.

The girls protested past the Andersons, who were another kind of Protestant with only two kids in the family. Mary Clare was glad nobody was outside. But when they passed the Healy house, some of the kids were playing on the porch and two of them joined the protest. By the time they got home, even Mary Clare was humming along.

She ushered Margaret and Gabriella straight through the house to the upstairs bathroom, where they handed over their blouses to Mary Clare. She used bar soap and cold water to work the stains, all the while thinking about Sister Agnes and the bill she dreaded showing her parents.

No! She stamped her foot, though no one was near to appreciate the effect. She wouldn't, *couldn't* burden her parents with another bill. She had to figure out how to get the money herself.

Mary Clare locked the door and ripped the envelope open. It was not only a sin to disobey Sister, but it was probably a crime to open someone else's mail. The image of her standing behind bars in a striped uniform made her hesitate for a minute. A jail cell was not the image of a saint she'd had in mind. But, she reasoned, she wasn't going to get caught, and as far as the sin went — well, it was for the good of her family. A sin that was for the good of the family shouldn't count.

The bill was straightforward, but the note penned in red ink made her want to scream. "We do not have the means to provide charity for Gabriella's First Communion supplies. This must be paid by Monday or Gabriella will have to go without."

Mary Clare ripped the bill into little tiny pieces and dropped them in the toilet. She flushed twice. Watching the last of the pieces swirl in the toilet bowl, she stopped, paralyzed. Where was she going to get the money? She pictured the look on Sister Agony's face — disgust. Disgust that her family didn't have the money! The image vanquished all anxiety and brought back angry determination. She'd give up the money she'd been saving to buy a transistor radio to take to the lake this summer: all $2.94. She'd throw in the two cents from her penny loafers. She'd sell her angel collection. Well, maybe not the kissing angels her dad gave her when she was five, but everything else.

Mary Clare checked the bathroom floor to make sure she'd left no evidence. She braced herself. She didn't know how, just yet, but she was on a mission to collect every penny for Gabriella's First Communion.

Mary Clare O'Brian
188 Jackson Street
Littleburg, Wisconsin 53538

Saint Mary Magdalene Convent
1123 Good Shepherd Road
Minneapolis, Minnesota 55199

April 2, 1967

Dear Reverend Mother,

I bet you just got my first letter and you haven't had time to respond to it yet. I know that mother superiors are very busy. But I wanted to write another letter right away because I have more questions. I hope you don't mind. I'm also kind of scared that you've gotten a bad impression of me from my first letter. I'm really not a conceited person, but my mother always says "Mary Clare, recognize what you're good at, and the things you're not good at." I think she's right. That's why I told you about the things that will make me a good mother superior.

    Anyway, the question I have is about having babies. Don't worry, I know all about the birds and the bees — which is one of the reasons I want to become a nun! I know babies are a gift from God, but if a family already has more kids than they can afford, shouldn't they stop having babies? I overheard Mom and two of her friends saying that the Church won't let them take the new birth control pill. Why not?

Very Sincerely,
Mary Clare O'Brian

P.S. I've been thinking about the name of your convent. Did you name it Mary Magdalene because she was a prostitute who reformed, and you want the unwed mothers to reform like she did?

P.P.S. My parish is St. Maria Goretti. She died for her virginity. I don't know any mothers who became saints, so why does the Church want married women to have so many babies?

3

The next morning, Mary Clare did a thorough money search through the house. She racked up some loose change (along with five white lies—venial, not mortal sins—because nosey brothers and sisters wanted to know what she was looking for). She searched under the frayed couch cushions and even moved the couch to look underneath (twenty-seven cents). She searched in all the inside suit pockets in her parents' closet (ninety-two cents) and even under their bed. She couldn't take the money on her father's dresser, because that was stealing. The laundry room, her final stop, turned out to be worth her time. Two clean dimes shined up at her from the inside of the dryer, and she discovered another five cents when going through pockets in the dirty clothes.

Mary Clare counted her money in the privacy of the upstairs bathroom: $1.44. Pretty good for not doing much of anything. That added to her radio savings ($2.94) and penny loafer pennies meant she had $4.40 toward the bill. She had a lot more work to do. If only Matthew were home from the seminary this weekend. She could talk to him about all of it—another baby on the way and how depressed Mom was about it. How frightening it was to see Mom falling apart. Sister Agony being so mean about Gabriella's First Communion money. She might even be brave enough to tell him about destroying the bill Sister gave her. Matthew was smart. He might have some idea how to help.

"Mary Clare!" her mother hollered up the stairs. "Come help me make lunch!"

Mary Clare hurried to help. Her mother's eyes were red-rimmed, and she was still in a nightgown at almost noon. But at least she was making lunch. Mary Clare gave her mother a quick hug and pulled out a butter knife to help with the sandwiches.

Together they made fourteen peanut butter and banana sandwiches, a family favorite. Mary Clare spread the peanut butter and her mother followed with sliced bananas.

"I think we'd better add a few peanut butter and jelly," Mary Clare said, pausing to look out the back door. "Some of the Healy and Murphy kids are playing over, and I don't think they eat peanut butter and banana." Her mother nodded and set to work slicing a third loaf of the bread she'd baked yesterday morning.

"I'm not surprised," her mother said. "It's like June out there."

Mary Clare slopped some jelly on her T-shirt. Her mother saw it and sighed. "You're going to have to change that before going to confession."

"I *will*," Mary Clare snapped. Why did her mother have to say something about every little thing?

As she carried the plates of sandwiches out to the yard, she got to thinking about how many neighbor kids were always around. Why not have some kind of a sale — Kool-Aid, cookies, lemon bars, something like that?

"Come and get it!" she yelled once her mother put down red-checkered tablecloths on the two picnic tables. They'd added chips and Kool-Aid to the sandwiches.

The kids crowded around the table and devoured the food.

While they were chattering and eating, Mary Clare whispered her idea to her mother, who shrugged and nodded.

"As long as you pay for anything we don't have in the house," her mom said.

She made a quick decision on what to sell so she could catch the kids before they ran off to play. Mary Clare turned to the noisy group and whistled.

"Everybody, tomorrow afternoon I'm having a lemonade and cookie sale," she said. "Spread the word!"

She answered the stream of questions that followed.

"Five cents," she told Sandy Healy.

"Surprise cookies," she told Anne. ("Surprise cookies" meant she had to find out what ingredients were in the house.)

"No, just two kinds of cookies," she told Teeny Freeman.

"Two o'clock," she told Margaret. "After church and Sunday brunch."

After lunch and cleanup, Mary Clare helped get the little kids down for a nap. By the time everyone was asleep it was time to get ready for confession. She would be relieved to get all those sins off her soul—especially flushing the bill down the toilet.

"Is everybody ready?" Mary Clare's father asked. "Boys, off that couch. Don't think you're getting out of confession."

"Dad, other kids don't have to go every single week," Mark complained.

"You're not other kids."

Mary Clare and Luke mouthed their father's familiar words to each other as they traipsed to the car.

"Move over!" Mark snapped at Mary Clare. He was a junior in high school, tall, dark, and handsome, and a star football player. But at home he could be really bossy, especially when Dad made him do things like go to confession every Saturday.

Mary Clare obliged, but not until she added, "Now you have to confess being rude."

Mark suggested she had to confess being a big mouth.

"Okay, everybody think about your own sins, and try being quiet like Anne," Dad said.

Mary Clare wasn't quite done thinking about Mark's sins. She envisioned that awful picture of Dante's Inferno Dad had in his office. It showed the horrors of hell—people burning, getting stabbed by pitchforks, freezing, their faces distorted in agony. She imagined Mark in hell, begging Saint Mary Clare to intercede with God for mercy. Since she'd be a saint, she'd have a direct connection to God. Mary Clare imagined herself in her light, heavenly body, looking down on Mark as he suffered. She didn't want him to be in pain, but he *had* been pretty mean to her on earth. But here in heaven, she was filled with love. Just as she was forgiving him for his earthly transgressions, she felt a sharp pain on her arm.

"Move over," Mark demanded. "You're taking up too much space."

Mary Clare squished over in the seat as much as she could to give him room, but she glared at her brother. *Fine*, she thought, *he can just rot in hell.*

Suddenly it occurred to her that these thoughts were probably sins. Saints, most likely, didn't enjoy images of their brothers suffering in hell. But, then, none of the saints had *her* brothers. She made a mental note to add this to her confession anyway.

When they arrived at Saint Maria Goretti Church, Mary Clare followed their father to a pew on the left side. They knelt to examine their consciences and prepare for a thorough and sincere confession. But Mary Clare was more interested in watching the people in line and figuring out which priest was in which confessional. It wasn't hard. One look told Mary Clare that Father Williams was on the left side and Father Dwyer was on the right. The line was short on Father Williams' side, but it moved far more slowly than Father Dwyer's longer line. When an elderly man Mary Clare didn't recognize stepped out of Father Williams' confessional, he looked stricken. Father Williams was old, cranky, and hard of hearing. He'd say, "What?" and, "Come again?" to the sweating penitent behind the curtain. Mary Clare remembered her experience with Father Williams. She had to speak so loudly she feared everyone in the pews and the next confessional could hear.

Mark and Luke had already gone to the other side of church and taken positions in Father Dwyer's line when Mary Clare got up and followed. He was a young priest popular for his light penances and kind spirit. Mary Clare liked him a lot. Besides, her father had just gotten into Father Williams' line and she wasn't about to get behind him. He took forever in the confessional. And he would have to talk so loud she might hear his sins.

Mary Clare used to think her dad wasn't as organized as she was. Maybe he didn't have his sins written down ahead of time and had to think up each one while he was inside the confessional. She tried to imagine what his list of sins would be. He yelled too much, that was for sure. And sometimes he disciplined the wrong kid because he was too mad to find out what was going on. He fought with her mom a lot. But saying those sins wouldn't take up all the time he was in the confessional. Mary Clare worried that people thought he was the biggest sinner in the whole parish.

The part she couldn't explain was his penance. While Father Dwyer usually gave her a few Hail Mary's and Glory Be to the Father's to say, Mary Clare's father prayed forever. The kids had learned long ago that part of their penance was waiting an eternity in the vestibule for their dad to finish praying.

When a sinner knelt in the confessional, a little light on the outside shone red. This meant it was occupied. But the minute the penitent stood to leave, the light turned green, which meant that the next person in line could go in. Now Mary Clare took her turn. Once inside, she closed the heavy curtain and Father Dwyer slid open a small window, leaving a grate between them. This way they could hear one another without the priest identifying the sinner.

"Bless me Father, for I have sinned. My last confession was one week ago." She removed the dog-eared slip of paper from her missal and began reading her list. "I talked in class approximately thirty-five times. I fought with my brothers and sisters three to five times a day, but mostly it was their fault, Father. I lied to my parents twice—but they were little white lies. I enjoyed imagining my brother in hell. I disobeyed Sister Agnes once but it was for a very good reason. And I opened up a piece of my parents' mail."

"Tell me about those last two, Mary Clare."

Mary Clare took in a sharp breath and let it out along with all the rest of the breath she'd been holding. "How do you know who this is, Father?" She could hear Father Dwyer cough. It sounded fake.

"You're my only parishioner who defends her sins while confessing them." He paused. "It's hard to make a good act of contrition when you're arguing."

"Yes, Father," Mary Clare said.

"Now, back to disobeying Sister and opening your parents' mail."

"Well, it's actually disobeying Sister *by* opening my parents' mail. I wasn't sure if that counted as one sin or two. I thought it would be safer to get absolution for both."

"Go on," Father said.

"Well, Father, Sister Agnes gave me a bill for Gabriella's First Communion stuff. But I couldn't give it to my parents because — because they don't have money and it would just make Mom cry again and Dad pace up and down. So I flushed it down the toilet. I don't really think it's fair to count this as a sin at all, because I did it for a worthy cause."

"How much was the bill?" Father asked.

"What?" Mary Clare returned.

"How much do you need for Gabriella's First Communion things?"

"The bill is $12.50," Mary Clare said. She could hear Father rustling around behind the wall. Suddenly the little trap door in the middle of the grate opened up and Father slid several dollars and a quarter through to Mary Clare's side.

"Here you go, Mary Clare. Some money toward Gabriella's bill. It's all I've got on me. Now, I absolve you of your sins. For your penance say three Our Fathers, three Hail Mary's, and three Glory Be's. Make a good Act of Contrition. And for heaven's sake don't argue with God while you're doing it. And don't go spreading it around that I gave you money."

Mary Clare floated out of the confessional and levitated to the nearest pew. She couldn't believe what Father had just done. She opened her missal and counted the money. Six dollars and twenty-five cents. Mary Clare's smile filled her entire face. God was going halfsies.

Saint Mary Magdalene Convent and School
1123 Good Shepherd Road
Minneapolis, Minnesota 55199

Mary Clare O'Brian
188 Jackson St.
Littleburg, Wisconsin 53538

April, 1967

Dear Mary Clare,

I received your very interesting letter and have been giving it prayerful thought ever since. In that letter you indicated that you wanted to become the Mother Superior of the order. You asked how you could apply for my job, you gave me a list of your qualifications for the position, you commented on how much you liked our habits, and you mentioned your hurry to get into the convent right after the eighth grade. I will do my best to respond.

There are several steps a young girl takes when she enters Mary Magdalene Convent. She begins as a postulant, learning about the religious life. Then she becomes a novice. After two years she takes temporary vows of poverty, chastity, and obedience and receives the habit. Final vows are taken three years after that, when she knows she is truly ready. In her early training she is mostly silent as she listens to God and learns His will.

Our sisters are working nuns. We teach, we nurse, we do missionary work. St. Mary Magdalene Convent, as you already know, works with troubled girls who are unwed mothers. We take care of the babies until we find good families to adopt them.

Each year we get hundreds of inquiries about the application process, but I must say, in the twenty-one years I've been Mother

Superior, I have never had anyone ask me how she could take over my job! The mother superior is elected by the other sisters. She is usually a seasoned nun—age forty or over. Candidates are nominated by the other sisters and after prayerful consideration we hold a vote. In the history of our convent, no one has ever campaigned for the position. Because we pray, we trust that God has a hand in choosing the mother superior and that she will make decisions according to God's will. But the skills you've developed in campaigning may be useful in serving God in other ways.

Like you, I am quite fond of St. Theresa the Little Flower. Did you know that she wrote an autobiography called The Interior Castle? You might want to try reading it. She has much to teach all of us about serving God humbly.

You must ask yourself, Mary Clare, what makes you want to become a nun? What do the vows of poverty, chastity, and obedience mean to you? Pray to God for a sign that you have a vocation. Then listen in your heart for the answer. Pray for greater humility and a deepening of your faith. Then after high school, if you feel God's calling, you can apply to a convent of your choice. St. Mary Magdalene Convent only accepts candidates who are at least eighteen years of age. In the meantime, it's fine for you to like boys. If you have a true vocation, you will know if God is calling you, even with boys in your life.

In God's love,
Mother Monica
Saint Mary Magdalene Convent and School

4

"April showers bring May flowers," Anne was singing as she watched the sky empty itself in torrents out the bedroom window.

Mary Clare sat up straight in her bed. "Oh *no*," she said, thinking about the dozens of molasses and chocolate chip cookies she had baked last night for her sale today. She had even spent forty cents of the money she'd already collected as an investment in the chocolate chips. But if it kept raining like this, she could forget earning the rest of the money for Gabriella's First Communion supplies before tomorrow. She still needed $2.25.

"You look funny," Anne said.

Mary Clare turned to look in the mirror. She had rolled her hair in soup cans to try, once again, to straighten it. Instead, the cans cluttered her bed and the floor, except the two that dangled off the left side of her head. The rest of her hair was just as curly as could be. Maybe it was a sign that God wanted her to become a nun and cover it up, once and for all. A saint would let go of her pride. The best Mary Clare could do was to offer her humiliation up to Jesus.

"You look funny too," she said to Anne, who had wrapped

herself in the white lace curtains so only her freckled face and blue eyes were visible. "You look like a fancy kind of nun."

"I wish nuns really did wear lace veils," Anne said.

"Good idea," Mary Clare said. She made a mental note to remember lace veils in case she decided to start her own convent. She had been thinking about that. If she started her own convent she would be the Mother Superior for certain. Saint Clare had started her own convent, and that was probably why she got made into a saint. The idea was becoming her backup plan in case she couldn't get the job as a Good Shepherd nun.

Mary Clare watched as Anne twisted the curtains tighter. "If you pull those curtains down you'll be in big trouble," she said.

The storm made it so dark outside that Mary Clare wanted to crawl back in bed and pull the covers over her head. But it was already 9:30 according to the alarm clock on her dresser. She wondered why her mother hadn't called her to help get the kids ready for the 11:00 Mass. Mary Clare reluctantly collected the cans that had failed to straighten her hair and meandered down the stairs. She found her mother in the kitchen reading a book by Betty Freidan. The kitchen smelled like coffee and cigarettes and whatever sweet thing was in the oven. By the looks of the full ashtray in front of her, it appeared that her mother had been sitting there for quite some time. Mary Clare winced when she saw her mother's red-rimmed eyes. When she reached for her coffee cup, Mary Clare stopped her.

"Mom, what are you doing? You forgot to fast for Communion!" Her mother looked up briefly at the clock, then turned her attention back to her book. This was so different from the way her mother used to be. Her mother was so careful that everyone remembered to fast before Mass, she'd tie rags around the faucets to remind them.

"I'm not going," her mother said.

Mary Clare looked at her mom carefully. She didn't look like she was dying or anything. Missing Sunday Mass was a sin. Mary Clare pulled up a chair next to her mother to get a better look. Her mother had no makeup on and was wearing old — practically ragged — maternity clothes. Other than the red-rimmed eyes, she just looked sad.

"Mom, are you sick?"

"Sort of," her mother answered. She hoisted herself up from the chair and waddled over to the oven, as if she'd already gained her usual thirty pounds in her pregnancy. "Sick and tired," she murmured under her breath. "Just sick and tired."

Now Mary Clare was frightened. Her mother was losing her faith. Sister Regina, Mary Clare's third grade teacher, had warned about this. How adults sometimes just wandered away from their faith and could be lost, forever, to the Kingdom of Heaven. She couldn't let that happen.

"Mom, you have to …"

Mary Clare's mother slammed the pan of poppy-seed coffee cake she'd retrieved from the oven onto the top of the cooling rack.

"Don't you tell me what I 'have to,' Mary Clare! I have been doing what I 'have to' my entire life, and I won't have you or your father or … even the Church tell me what I 'have to' do."

Mary Clare nodded. She didn't think her shocked vocal chords could manage a peep just then. She noticed the bookmark in *The Feminine Mystique*. Her mother was halfway through it. And from the number of cigarette butts in the ashtray, it looked like she had been reading all night. Could that book be stealing her mother's faith?

This was the very reason the Holy Catholic Church sent lists home of "approved" and "prohibited" shows to watch on television. She hadn't seen one yet, but there had to be lists of prohibited books as well. She would have to find a way to read that book to find out what was happening to her mother.

"I'm sorry, Mary Clare. I didn't mean to take it out on you." Her mother wrapped Mary Clare in a vanilla-and-tobacco-and-coffee-smelling hug. "Now, be my angel and run down to the basement to get a pair of Martha's underpants from the dryer. She put on her own dress but told me she didn't have clean underwear."

Mary Clare did as she was told, but once downstairs she decided to fold the whole load of clothes. Each member of the family had either a basket or box for clean clothes, and Mary Clare carefully separated each item into the right pile. When she was almost finished, her mother called to her.

"I'm running Luke over to church. He's serving at the eleven o'clock Mass. Please get Johnny dressed—it's getting late."

Mary Clare ran back upstairs, forgetting about the underpants. She still had to get herself dressed and was running out of time.

●

"Your mother's not feeling well," Dad said as he ushered Mark, Mary Clare, Anne, Gabriella, Margaret, Martha, and Johnny into the car. Matthew had stayed at the seminary this weekend, but it was still just as crowded. Mary Clare asked if all the girls had remembered head coverings for church, but the question got lost in Margaret and Martha's squabble over who had to sit on the floor.

By the time Dad had let them out at the front door so they wouldn't all get drenched, Mass had already begun. They stood in the vestibule waiting for their father to park the car and join them. Even the short distance from the car to the door had left them wet.

"They're at the confiteor already," Mark hissed through closed teeth. He glared. "This is so embarrassing."

Mary Clare looked out over the congregation. Sure enough, they were reciting the prayer that asked God to forgive their sins. She was embarrassed too, but she was too busy checking all the kids to give into it just then. "Where's your chapel veil?" she hissed at Gabriella. Gabriella shrugged. Mary Clare made the girls search their pockets but they came up empty-handed. Finally Mary Clare pulled a Kleenex from her pocket. She found a bobby pin to attach it to Gabriella's head.

Mark rolled his eyes. "From now on I'm walking to Mass," he proclaimed just as their father walked through the door.

"You can start by walking home today," he said.

Mark glanced nervously at the rain, but then his face hardened. "Fine," he said.

Going into church late made Mark angry every time. The early birds always took the middle pews and people worked their way back from there. By the time Mary Clare's family arrived, the only seats left would be in the front of the church. A somber usher would walk them past row after row of the congregation, who would turn from prayer to watch the motley O'Brians make their way to the front of the church. Today there was only one pew in front of them.

The minute the priest started saying the Gloria, Mary Clare knew what was about to happen. She turned to see Anne and Gabriella mouthing the words to the popular Van Morrison song. "Gloria. G-L-O-R-I-A. GLORIA!" Mark snickered, but Mary Clare and her father glared at the girls. Mary Clare tried not to think about how many people behind them were staring.

Gradually, Mary Clare pulled her attention away from her family and into the service. But when Father Williams started the sermon, she decided to pray rather than try to follow what he was saying. Even Saint Theresa would have had trouble listening. She prayed that her mother would not lose her faith, and that she would be okay with having another baby. She prayed for God to bring her family enough money, for her parents and all her brothers and sisters, for the pagan babies and unpopular kids and the poor souls in purgatory. She thanked God that the long winter was over and that they would soon be out of school and able to go swimming every day. She prayed to win the essay contest on vocations so she'd know that God accepted her deal to take care of her family if she became a saint. Finally, she asked God to inspire her to find a way to get the two dollars and twenty-five cents she still needed to turn in to Sister Agony.

She was abruptly pulled out of prayer when Johnny dropped his picture prayer book over the pew and practically fell over trying to get it from the floor in front of them. As Mary Clare pulled him back, Martha tried to retrieve it. She bent over the pew as far as she could, revealing a *bare bottom*! There was an audible gasp from the row behind them, followed by whispers and giggles. Mark pulled Martha roughly back to her seat. Mary Clare hadn't seen his face so red since the boys played cowboys and Indians years before and Mark painted his face like a warrior.

Underpants! Mary Clare remembered far too late. That's what she had gone downstairs to get.

Then Johnny started to cry because he wanted his book, Martha cried because Mark had been mean to her, and Gabriella took off the Kleenex she was wearing as a hair covering to wipe both of their tears. Mary Clare got the two kids to smile at Luke, who looked angelic in his server's garb but was looking anxiously at his family. When he saw that Johnny and Martha were smiling at him, he wiggled his ears in that hilarious way of his. Both kids laughed and stopped crying. Unfortunately, most of the congregation laughed too, which made Father Williams furrow his eyebrows and raise his voice as he consecrated the host.

Mary Clare lowered her eyes and prayed with her whole heart to be invisible. It didn't work. She didn't dare look at her father, who she knew would be furious, or Mark, who would be mortified.

After Mass, Mary Clare was grateful that the family was in the front of the church. It meant that they would be the last people out of the sanctuary and wouldn't have to talk to anyone. But a few of her parents' friends waited for them in the vestibule. Mary Clare ignored the adults and held Martha's hand tight. She was surprised when she heard laughter and realized it was coming from Mr. Zimmerman. "It certainly made for a memorable service," he was saying to her father. She looked up to see her father's angry look relax into a smile. Maybe his mood would soften now.

As the family raced through the parking lot traffic to avoid getting drenched, Mary Clare commented that Mark had left immediately after Communion.

"Where's Mark?" Anne asked.

"Walking," Mary Clare and their father chorused.

"If we pass him on the way we'll pick him up," Dad said. Mary Clare was relieved to hear the tenderness in his voice. She hoped they'd pick him up within the first block or two.

But they didn't see him on the way home. They didn't talk about what happened in church, either, because Johnny wailed the whole time. He was wet and hungry and didn't want to sit on anybody's lap, which wasn't possible considering how crowded the car was.

As Mary Clare was setting the table for Sunday brunch, she caught a glimpse of a soaked Mark racing up the stairs. But by the time they were ready to eat, Mark joined them in dry clothes. He sat as far away from Dad as possible, which meant he had to wait for each platter of scrambled eggs, sliced ham, and poppy seed coffee cake to get to his side of the table. "Can't you guys pass a little faster?" he complained while Martha struggled with the mechanics of getting a spoonful of eggs on her plate. "Everything's gonna be cold."

Martha pouted. Mary Clare was ready to jump up and help her but Mark got to her first. He smiled at Martha to show he wasn't mad at her. He heaped way too many eggs on her plate and then, seeing the surprised look on her face, put half back. Martha laughed.

"I'm wearing underpants now," she reassured Mark.

"Good," Mark said, and smiled at his youngest sister a second time.

By the time brunch was over and cleanup complete, the rain had stopped. It was still far too wet and sloppy to set up a table outside, and Mary Clare had pretty much given up on selling cookies when a few neighborhood kids started showing up. Mary Clare sold six cookies sitting behind the kitchen table. Thirty cents. Not even enough to cover the chocolate chips she'd bought. Still, she had pulled together $10.55 out of the $12.50 she needed.

She ended up giving cookies to everybody in the family, and because she felt desperate about the $1.95 she still needed, she ate a few herself.

When Mary Clare went to her room to rest off the awful feeling of too many cookies and monetary doom, all of her glow-in-the-dark statues were lined up on the dresser glowing. At first she was irritated. She wondered how the little kids had gotten up to the shoe box she kept them in on the highest shelf in the closet. But as she looked at them all lined up, Mary Clare had a brilliant idea. Forget selling cookies. She could have a different kind of sale—a private sale—where she'd invite only the kids who would benefit most from owning one or two of the glow-in-the-dark statues she'd gotten from the nuns over the years. It would be both a sacrifice and "good works."

The Healy twins would be good candidates. They were Catholic but surely neither had ever gotten an A in conduct, and she remembered Billy eying one of her statues wistfully. That was a while ago—maybe in third grade—but they still might want to buy one. But it was the public school kids in the neighborhood who she thought would most benefit. There were Tina Anderson and Becky Turner. Neither was Catholic but they were in the same grade as Mary Clare. They lived down the hill with just one house in between each other. Then there were the DeLuca kids, who lived across the street in the Southern-style white house with the rambling porch and didn't go to any church at all. She considered Joannie Marino, who was also in her class and did go to Saint Maria Goretti School. She probably had tons of glow-in-the-dark statues because she was so shy she hardly ever opened her mouth. If Mary Clare was selling angels from her collection, she'd consider contacting Joannie. But she wasn't. She couldn't. She loved them too much.

Mary Clare surrounded the lamp on her dresser with the statues and turned it on so they'd glow even brighter. Then she ran downstairs to the kitchen and started making phone calls. The Healy boys were gone, but she got hold of both Tina and Becky. She invited them over for cookies and they said they'd be right up.

Mary Clare ran downstairs to find that somebody had gotten into the cookies she'd hidden in the pots and pans cupboard. And she had given the kids a whole plate of cookies! At least they'd left enough so she could still serve her friends. Mary Clare placed the last of the cookies on a plate as the front doorbell was ringing.

"Who rang the doorbell?" Mom hollered from the basement.

"It's Tina and Becky for me. We'll be in my room for a while."

"Okay," Mom said. And the three girls were off to her room.

"Wow!" Tina exclaimed when she saw how the statues glowed in the dark.

"Isn't that something!" Becky added.

Mary Clare was heartened by their reactions.

"Let's see this one," Tina said. She held up the statue of St. Theresa, the Little Flower of Jesus. St. Theresa was holding a bouquet of pink roses. Before taking Tina and Becky to the closet where the statues would *really* glow, Mary Clare explained about the roses falling from the sky after St. Theresa's death.

"Talk about flower power!" Becky said.

Mary Clare laughed. She had seen the flower children on television holding signs that said "Make love not war." How funny to think of the term in relation to St. Theresa — or any saint, for that matter.

Tina reached for the last molasses cookie. When Becky objected, she divided it in two and gave Becky half. Becky picked up the statue of St. Theresa.

The girls were responding exactly the way Mary Clare hoped they would. "I'm selling those," she said.

"How much?" Becky asked with a mouth full of cookie.

"Twenty cents each," Mary Clare said.

Tina and Becky gave each other looks that Mary Clare couldn't quite decipher.

"That's too much," Becky said.

"Yeah," Tina added. "No deal."

Tina set down the St. Theresa statue on the dresser and Becky set the Virgin Mary next to it.

"Look, it's already losing its glow," Becky said.

Mary Clare had to act quickly if she wanted to make a sale.

She thought about what she'd read in the Baltimore Catechism the night before.

"Look, do you two know what indulgences are?" she asked.

They looked at each other. "No," they said.

"Well," Mary Clare started, "if you say certain prayers each day, you get time off of Purgatory. For example, if you say 'O Mary, conceived without sin, pray for us who have recourse to thee' every day for a month, you get three hundred days off of Purgatory! If you look at the statue every day, it will help you remember to say the prayer."

"What was that prayer again?" Becky asked. Mary Clare repeated the words and watched Becky's forehead wrinkle as she said them.

"I don't even know what that means," Becky said.

Tina shrugged her shoulders. "Me neither."

Mary Clare explained. "The Virgin Mary was born without original sin and we're asking her to pray to God for us."

"Original sin?" Becky asked. "What's that?"

"Why don't you just pray to God yourself?" Tina asked.

Mary Clare sighed. She couldn't believe how little non-Catholics knew about theology. It was probably because they didn't get religion classes in school. This was going to take time and patience, and she might not sell her statues today.

"I'm not sure my church even believes in Purgatory," Becky said.

Mary Clare wanted to argue. She wanted to say that it didn't matter what they believed, the Catholic Church was the *true* religion. She wanted to say that Purgatory was a fact, not a belief. She wanted to tell them that—that—that she didn't know why you prayed through the Virgin Mary and not directly to God, but that was just the way it was.

"God gives us mysteries," she said. "Mysteries to test our

faith." Mary Clare thought she sounded a little like Father Dwyer when he gave a sermon. It felt good. "We don't have to know *why* we pray through Mary or *why* we get three hundred days off of purgatory for saying that prayer every day for a month. We just have to believe and trust in the Lord. When I have doubts, I just remember that God tests us and that my faith has to win out."

"Mary Clare," Becky said, wearing a serious expression, "you're weird."

Tina giggled. "You really are, Mary Clare. You could be a minister."

"Or the Flying Nun on television—giving sermons," Becky added.

The balloon inside Mary Clare, the one with faith-filled ardor, burst in a flash of pain. She pictured her own face on the Flying Nun instead of Sally Fields' face. She pictured flying around giving sermons from the sky and couldn't help laughing along with Becky and Tina.

"Can we please change the subject?" Tina asked.

And they did. They talked about Mary Clare's Paul McCartney poster and who had which Beatles records. Mary Clare had a few singles but didn't have her own record player. She had to listen to them in the living room, so they decided not to bother. But when Becky said she had the new Sonny and Cher single "The Beat Goes On," they tried to remember the words and sing it. Between the three of them, they got almost the whole song.

For the next hour Mary Clare actually forgot about the money she needed and trying to be a saint. They were only interrupted twice: once by her mother, who wanted to remind Mary Clare that there was no eating in the bedrooms, and once by Margaret, who needed a change of clothes because hers had gotten dirty in the wet sandbox.

When Tina and Becky were about to leave, Tina asked to

buy the Virgin Mary statue after all, but only if she could get it for a dime. "My brother is going to Vietnam," she said. "And I'm gonna pray every day that he doesn't get hurt."

"Really?" Mary Clare said. "Didn't he graduate last year?"

Tina nodded. "He was working at the chicken plant and got drafted."

"Wow! I don't know anybody else in Vietnam," Mary Clare said. "I'll write down the indulgence too. But the indulgence can only be for the person praying, not for another person—unless they're dead."

Tina's eyes filled, and Mary Clare felt like an idiot. She hugged her friend. "I'll pray for him," she said. "Every day."

"As religious as you are, that should work!" Becky said.

Tina laughed, and Mary Clare laughed in relief.

"I'll pray too," Becky added. "How about you sell me St. Theresa—for a dime."

"Sold!" Mary Clare said.

Tina pointed to Mary Clare's angel collection on the high shelf above her Paul McCartney poster. "I'll give you forty cents for the kissing angels."

Mary Clare shook her head.

"Fifty cents, then. That's my final offer. C'mon. You've got about thirty others up there."

Mary Clare was torn. She needed the money but ... not the kissing angels. She shook her head. "You can have any other angels, but those are the ones my dad gave me when I was five."

"I remember," Becky said. "You broke your arm really bad, and he gave them to you for learning to write with your right hand because the doctors didn't think you'd ever use the left hand again."

Mary Clare nodded. "It was a miracle. Even the doctor cried when I could use it again."

"I still want them," Tina said. "Sixty cents."

Mary Clare wanted to cry, but she steeled herself. Sacrifice was painful. She would offer it up to God, like St. Theresa always did.

"Deal," she said, before she could chicken out.

Mary Clare O'Brian
188 Jackson Street
Littleburg, Wisconsin 53538

Sister Monica, Mother Superior
Saint Mary Magdalene Convent
1123 Good Shepherd Road
Minneapolis, Minnesota 55199

April 9, 1967

Dear Reverend Mother,

It's Mary Clare O'Brian again. Thanks for writing back. You sure gave me lots of stuff to think about. Is it okay if I keep writing? I have loads of questions and the more I think, the more questions I have.

I think that humility and humiliation are not the same. My family sometimes humiliates me, but humility is when you are modest about something. Right? I have been practicing humility all evening. I think I just about have it down. From now on when I walk into church, I'll bow my head just a little and hold my missal against my stomach with my hands folded over it just the way the nuns do. I think the effect will be best if I wear a mantilla instead of a chapel veil. The mantilla is much longer. Mine is white and lacy. I tried walking with my head bowed at home tonight, but when I ran into the guitar my brother Luke had propped against the wall he yelled at me to watch where I was going. He's not religious.

Also when people tell me I'm pretty or smart or good at something, instead of smiling and saying "thank you," I'll lower my eyes and say "No, I'm not."

I tried to get *The Interior Castle* by St. Theresa but it was checked out. I'll look for it at home, too. We have a million books.

I was thinking about the unwed mothers you work with. Do you think that having a child is a punishment from God because they were bad? My friend Kelly's mom said, "They made their bed, now they have to lie in it." But my mom said, "A baby is never a punishment." That confused me a little because Mom cried buckets when she found out she was having another baby. I was just wondering what you think.

I think there are two kinds of Catholics — old-fashioned and modern-day. Sister Agnes is an example of the old-fashioned kind. (We call her Sister Agony behind her back.) When she reminds us that God is JUST, her eyes get hard. She thinks we should suffer for Jesus, and her mouth puckers like she just ate something sour when anyone mentions the changes because of Vatican II. She thinks the old ways of the Church are better.

Sister Charlotte, my sixth grade teacher, is the modern-day kind. She thinks that God is love and she thinks God wants us to live lives of joy. She loves Vatican II because she thinks it's time to make lots of changes in the Church. So I was wondering if the Good Shepherd Convent is more Sister Agony or Sister Charlotte.

One other thing. I'm very worried that my mother may be losing her faith. She didn't go to Mass Sunday, which I know is a mortal sin. I made her a huge Spiritual Bouquet promising to say seven rosaries, fifty Our Father's, and seventy-five prayers to St. Francis. Is there something else I can do for her?

I sure hope you'll write back — but only if you want to.

Very Sincerely,
Mary Clare O'Brian

P.S. Just a few more questions. How long do the babies stay at Good Shepherd before they get adopted? Do you get to pick the parents for the little babies? That would be exciting. Also, what happens to the girls after they have their babies?

P.P.S. I forgot to tell you that I'm also practicing silence. So far I can make it through a whole class, unless it's boring, and I can usually make it for an entire Mass. Outside of that I've gone twenty-two and a half minutes in complete silence. How about that? It's a good start, I think.

P.P.P.S. Does sign language count as silence? I was in *The Miracle Worker* about Helen Keller for the Community Theater and I've taught all my friends the finger language.

5

Sister Agony raised her eyebrows in surprise when Mary Clare brought her the envelope. She motioned Mary Clare to have a seat while she counted the cash.

Mary Clare could hardly believe that she was in front of Sister Agony with every penny of Gabriella's bill. She wanted to giggle. She wanted to jump for joy, but she kept a perfectly straight face.

After her friends left, Mary Clare had been too tired and sad about losing her angels to come up with any more ideas about making money, though she was still $1.25 short. But when she was laying out the kids' clothes for the next day, she remembered that she needed to get the hot lunch money from her mother for the week. That was when it hit her: the lunch tickets were $1.25 per kid for one week of lunches. If she sacrificed her lunches for one week, she'd have exactly enough money to pay the bill.

"I don't think I've ever seen quite so many dimes and nickels," Sister said. She frowned as she counted the change. When Sister was satisfied that the entire $12.50 was there, she pursed her lips. Mary Clare couldn't tell if Sister's furled forehead showed satisfaction or suspicion, but at the moment she didn't much care. Gabriella's First Communion bill was paid! Mary Clare had to bite the inside of her lip to keep a straight face when what she really wanted to do was shout hip hip hoorah!

Sister Agony said thank you at the exact same moment the morning bell rang, so Mary Clare didn't catch her tone of voice. Sister stood.

"Um, Sister," Mary Clare hesitated. "Could I please have a receipt?"

Sister looked like Mary Clare had slapped her in the face. She held open the notebook. "I've noted it right here, Mary Clare. That should be satisfactory."

Inside Mary Clare was a little shaky, but she made herself look confident. "My mother needs a receipt," she said. It was only a little white lie, she reasoned. Her white lies were always for the good. Mary Clare's mother *did* need a receipt. She needed to see that she had one less bill to worry about. Mary Clare imagined how she'd sneak the paid receipt into the house and try to find some uncluttered place where her mother would notice it. Her mother would probably think her father had paid it, and it would be one worry off her chest.

As Sister reluctantly pulled out a piece of paper and wrote, "First Communion supplies, $12.50, Gabriella O'Brian," Mary Clare hid the pride that was swelling up inside. Sister ruffled through her desk for the red ink pad and the right stamp. Finally she planted the stamp firmly on the receipt. PAID IN FULL. She reached across the desk to hand it to Mary Clare. Mary Clare took it. As she turned to leave the room, her skirt twirled and her penny loafers squeaked.

"Don't you want Gabriella's First Communion supplies?"

Mary Clare stopped. She turned around. She hadn't thought about actually receiving Gabriella's things. Sister reached under her desk and retrieved a plump paper bag with Gabriella's name stapled to the top. She produced a tight smile when she handed it to Mary Clare.

"Thank you, Sister," Mary Clare said, looking Sister Agony straight in the eye. "I'll be sure to give this to my mother as soon as I get home tonight." Mary Clare wanted to dance down the hallway, but she kept her composure. She couldn't wait until recess, when she'd take the bag into the bathroom and carefully remove the staple to look inside. She knew that the items were basically the same as all the kids received—a missal, a rosary, a decorated candle, and a cross or scapular to wear around the neck. But there were numerous styles and colors. And it brought back sweet memories of Mary Clare's own First Communion.

Mary Clare dropped off the bag in her locker. She looked up to see the DeLuca twins approaching from the other side. They smiled and gave her a quick wave, and she nodded toward them without smiling. She waited in the hallway, counting to sixty so no one would think she was with them, then clamored into the classroom where kids were chatting. She barely made it to her seat before the second bell rang.

In spite of her efforts, Kelly tapped her on the shoulder. "Did you walk to school with the DeLuca twins?" Mary Clare gave her a look that said *Don't be ridiculous.*

Sister clapped her hands to get everyone's attention, and Religion class was underway.

At morning recess Mary Clare returned to her locker and pulled off her blazer to hide the bag. When she was safely inside a stall in the girls' bathroom, she carefully removed the staple and peeked at the boxes inside. She knew the long one contained the same candle she had gotten on her own First Communion, so she didn't open that. The missal was beautiful, with a white leather cover and two green ribbons to mark different prayers or the Mass or songs. Inside, the words to the Mass were all in

English. This was a brand-new thing. Up until Pope John XXIII decided that the Mass should be in the language of the people, one side of the page was in Latin and the other in English.

Next, Mary Clare opened the rosary. It had its own case, white with a gold cross that said "My Rosary" on it. The rosary was made of rose stones. Mary Clare laughed. A rose rosary for Gabby Rose. Finally she opened the little box that contained a silver cross on a delicate chain. Mary Clare smiled. These would make Gabriella feel like a princess.

By the time she put everything away and returned the package to her locker, recess was over.

"Where were you?" Kelly asked when they were taking their seats in the classroom.

Mary Clare whispered that she had picked up Gabriella's First Communion things.

"Ahhh," Kelly said, her eyes sparkling. "Are they nice?"

Mary Clare shrugged. "I haven't seen them yet."

Even though Mary Clare's classroom was on the second floor and the lunch room was in the school basement, the food smells started torturing her by 10:00 a.m. She could smell something sweet and apple-ish from the lunch room. Dessert. Maybe they were serving warm apple strudel with whipped cream. Mary Clare's mouth watered. She hadn't even thought to bring a sandwich.

If only this were a sauerkraut day she'd be in good shape. Most everyone hated sauerkraut day, but Mary Clare couldn't understand why. The way the lunch ladies made it, it was a casserole. The bottom layer was pork, followed by a thick layer of sauerkraut and an even thicker layer of mashed potatoes. Delicious.

Students would start moaning even before the lunch ladies served their plates. Everyone got the same amount of food and everyone was expected to eat everything they were given. Waste was a sin. But plenty of kids would sin on sauerkraut day by stuffing the casserole in their milk cartons or napkins.

Mary Clare tried to help out as many friends as she could on sauerkraut day. Once she ate three lunches. It made her stomach hurt, but she was proud of her good work.

"I prevented you guys from committing the sin of wastefulness," she said.

"Thanks," Sandy said.

"Yeah, thanks," Jen said. Then she stopped. "Wait. You ate three meals at lunch. Isn't that the sin of gluttony?"

Mary Clare hadn't looked at it that way. But when her stomach had hurt all afternoon, she'd known Jen was right. She would have to confess gluttony and pray that she didn't throw up.

But this day was not a sauerkraut day. By 11:00, the smell of beef wafted through the air. By lunchtime she felt like crying. She didn't want to sit empty-plated with the hot-lunch kids, and she didn't want to sit with the bag-lunchers. The bag-lunchers consisted of four unpopular kids—Joannie Marino, Phil Flannagan, and the DeLuca twins, Peter and Paula. Her friends would wonder what she was doing on that side of the room. Plus she didn't have a bag lunch either.

So Mary Clare spent twenty minutes in the girls' bathroom feeling sorry for herself. When she could hear kids chatting outside the lunchroom and the heavy metal doors screeching open as kids went out on the playground, she let herself out of the stall and went outside, too.

"Mary Clare, play four square with us," Sandy said. But Mary Clare wasn't interested in four square. She was interested in roast beef and apple strudel. She moped around the playground.

"What's wrong?" Kelly asked.

"Nothing," Mary Clare answered.

"You missed a good lunch."

"I *know!*" Mary Clare snapped.

Kelly's eyes opened wide. She hesitated for a second. "I'm going to play four-square," she said, then ran off to join the group of kids on the blacktop in front of the school. Mary Clare watched as she whispered something to the other girls, and in a minute they were all looking at her as if she smelled bad.

Mary Clare leaned against the bicycle stand that stood between the convent and the school on the north side. There she could watch the little kids on the merry-go-round and see the boys playing basketball on the back playground. She wished she could explain the whole thing to her friends. They'd probably admire her for sacrificing lunch so her sister could have her First Communion things. But maybe they wouldn't. Maybe they'd feel superior to her, knowing that her family was that poor. If it wasn't for the beautiful clothes her mother made from fabrics she found on sale and the fact that they wore uniforms to school, the other kids would have found out a long time ago.

Becoming a saint is lonely, God. I hope you appreciate my sacrifice. I know I can't brag about it, because then I'd be getting my reward on earth instead of in Heaven, but I want you to see that I'm really, really trying. Please don't forget your part of the deal. I can't wait for Mom and Dad to have everything they need.

She kicked a pebble across the asphalt and watched it fly, and then skitter until it hit a black habit several yards away. Mary Clare followed the shoes upwards past the habit, until she saw that the habit was connected to Sister Agony. Sister Agony looked down at the pebble, then followed its path with her eyes until she was looking straight at Mary Clare. She had hit Sister Agony!

Mary Clare took in a breath. Sister Agony headed straight toward Mary Clare, her lips pinched, her eyes flashing.

"You kicked that stone at me, didn't you, Mary Clare?"

"No, Sister …" If Sister had let her finish she would have explained that she kicked the stone but not *at* Sister, that she didn't even know Sister was there. But Sister interrupted.

"Well, where did it come from?" Sister raised her hands to the sky. "Heaven?"

Mary Clare opened her mouth again, but Sister's arms were now spread wide like Christ on the cross. Her huge sleeves made her look like a bat. If the wind was blowing she could have been the Flying Nun. "I don't feel any wind," she said, "so the stone didn't *blow* over to hit me."

"No, Sister. It …" But Sister Agony wasn't finished. She pointed toward the kids behind Mary Clare, who had stopped playing and were watching them. "It came from this direction, so I know the students playing four-square didn't throw it."

Again Mary Clare opened her mouth to explain, but Sister was flapping her chubby index finger right in Mary Clare's face. "You'll spend your recesses for the rest of the week sweeping the blacktop," she thundered, then stomped away.

The reaction Mary Clare got from the other kids almost made the crime worth the punishment. The four-square kids surrounded her, quietly cheering her on.

"You got her," Jen said.

"That was a pretty big stone, too," Kelly said, admiring it.

"I wonder if it left a bruise," Sandy said. Her face looked puzzled. "If it's even possible for nuns to get bruises."

The bell rang. Word spread to the boys as they came in from the basketball courts in the back, and soon everyone was grinning and clapping her on the back. No one asked Mary Clare if she had kicked the stone on purpose or even why she had done it. Sister Agony had caused each one of them pain at one time or another, and they assumed her actions were intentional.

Good. She'd let them think what they wanted. She knew it was a sin feeling good about Sister getting hit, but she couldn't help it. After all, kicking Sister was an accident. But she felt good. She loved the attention from the other students. She loved the feeling that she had gotten Sister twice in one day—first by producing every penny for Gabriella's First Communion and demanding a receipt. Then by kicking Sister. The satisfaction she felt filled her up so much she could hardly tell she had missed lunch. If there was anything she needed to confess it was probably that.

Saint Mary Magdalene Convent and School
1123 Good Shepherd Road
Minneapolis, Minnesota 55199

Mary Clare O'Brian
188 Jackson St.
Littleburg, Wisconsin 53538

April, 1967

Dear Mary Clare,

I received your second letter soon after I responded to your first. In the second letter you expressed concern that I might think you were conceited. You also wanted to know if you could continue to write to me, and you raised some questions.

Yes, you can continue to write to me, and I will respond as long as we both feel that you are learning from our correspondence. I do not think of you as conceited, but as high spirited, confident, and sincere. But you have much to learn. Not very long ago, my job would have been to break your spirit so that it would be easier for you to be obedient to God. But I believe that you could do a great deal of good if that spirit of yours is channeled into God's work.

About humility. My dear Mary Clare, humility is not acting, but a way of being in the world. The person with humility should know her own strengths and recognize them for what they are—gifts from God. Then she should use those gifts to serve God. That doesn't mean you should strive to get my job just because you have leadership skills. Instead you should pray for direction and for the strength to serve God, no matter what is asked of you.

I'm sorry your mother is struggling with her pregnancy. Children are always blessings—even the babies of unwed mothers. Those

67

babies are blessings for people who can't have children of their own. You just wait. When your mother has her baby, you will all love that child as much as you love each other.

Now, about the two kinds of Catholics you talked about — old-fashioned and modern-day. It is, in fact, a tumultuous time in the Church. But if you think about how people are responding to the changes from Vatican II, you'll see that it's really more complicated than that. You yourself may find that you hold fast to some of the old Catholic traditions and at the same time welcome some of the reforms. Most of us are muddling through right now and asking for constant guidance as we look to building the Church of the future.

God bless you!
Mother Monica

P.S. Yes, we pick the adoptive parents. Babies stay for two weeks to a year. After the girls have their babies they go back to their lives, though a few apply to enter our convent.

No, you can't use sign language when practicing silence. You certainly are a creative one!

6

Mary Clare began each morning more determined than the last to be saintly in her thoughts, words, and actions. But usually she had racked up at least one sin before she even made it to school. Fighting with Mark and Luke was her biggest challenge, but lately she'd become more aware that her thoughts were not always charitable. Sometimes she even forgot that she was trying to become a saint and didn't think about her sins for hours. That worried her in particular. She knew she couldn't be perfect, but she did have to keep an accurate sin count. If she missed some at Saturday confession, she might still have blotches on her soul afterwards. And that's why God had stopped listening to her to begin with.

On Tuesday Mary Clare was prepared to keep better tabs on her sins. She had remembered that some saint or other had used pebbles to keep count, and she had decided to do the same. In the morning she placed ten pebbles in her right pocket (right for righteous) and forced herself to move one over to the left pocket each time she committed a sin. By lunchtime she had four sins: one for sneaking a peanut butter and jelly sandwich to school when she was supposed to be eating hot lunch, two for talking in class, and one for writing Kelly a note. But she would try to make up for these sins by making a big sacrifice. She was going to sit with the unpopular kids at lunch.

She approached their table with a broad smile and a cheerful "hello" and plopped herself down in the empty chair next to Joannie Marino. The four of them eyed each other, wearing expressions that looked like a bird had pooped in the middle of the table. No one said a word. She looked around the table at the blank expressions and pulled out her sandwich, though she'd lost her appetite. It had never occurred to Mary Clare that maybe the unpopular kids might not want *her* to sit with *them*.

They all focused on their lunches. Joannie Marino removed one item after another from her lunch bag and set it all before her as if she were putting it on a plate: an egg-salad sandwich, a Tupperware container of fruit cocktail, a chocolate cupcake in wax paper. Phil Flanagan briefly considered the hard-boiled egg in his bag and tossed it back in. He removed the wax paper from his peanut butter and jelly sandwich and started eating. The DeLuca twins opened containers of cold macaroni and cheese and started eating too.

"You like cold casserole?" Mary Clare asked.

Peter and Paula nodded.

She tried again. "How come you guys don't eat hot lunches? Don't you like them?"

Silence.

Finally Paula asked a question of her own. "How come you're eating with us today?"

"I thought the change would be nice," Mary Clare lied.

"Fat chance," Phil said. The other three laughed—even Joannie.

Mary Clare wished she could disappear. She had never felt so unwelcome.

"Hot lunches are fine," Peter said.

"It's the kids we can't stand," Paula added.

Joannie nodded, keeping her eyes focused on her sandwich. Phil laughed.

Mary Clare tried not to look as surprised and hurt as she felt. She broke off a tiny bite of her sandwich and put it in her mouth, but it was hard to swallow. Phil had laughed at her. Phil, who should have been in seventh grade instead of sixth but flunked fourth. Phil, who was always late for school and fell asleep in class all the time — sometimes even drooling. Phil, who was a farmer and smelled like a barn, was laughing at her.

She couldn't say anything because she had peanut butter stuck in her throat. She had never thought of these guys as friends. She had figured they stuck together with nothing more in common than their unlikeability. But the looks they were giving each other, like they enjoyed making her squirm, made it seem like they had secrets and inside jokes like a real group of friends.

"How are you doing on your essay for the diocesan contest?" Paula asked Joannie.

Joannie shrugged and made a so-so gesture with her hand. Mary Clare didn't know why Joannie was so quiet. She was tiny, with dirty blonde hair and a mousey voice that actually squeaked when she tried to answer a question in class. Mary Clare had been one of the kids who mocked Joannie by making squeaky noises when they passed her in the hall, but she hadn't done that for a long time, and she regretted doing it now.

"We haven't even started ours," Peter said. "But mine is gonna be about a paragraph long."

Mary Clare decided to jump in. "I've been thinking about mine. I just haven't put it down on paper yet."

"You'll win," Phil said.

Mary Clare momentarily forgot she was with kids who didn't like her. "You think so, really? I'd love to win!"

Paula and Joannie rolled their eyes.

"I'd *love* to win," Paula imitated in a fake voice.

Everyone except Mary Clare laughed. Her eyes stung, and she was sure she had a red face from the heat she could feel in it.

Paula spoke again, this time using her real voice. "Really, Peter and I would love to win but we have cooties, remember?"

The blow was harder than any physical hit. "It's been a long time since I said anything like that," Mary Clare said weakly.

"Fourth grade," Joannie said. Her eyes were teary.

Mary Clare thought of all the times she had slowed down or sped up on the walk to avoid walking with Joannie, even though she lived right across the street.

"I'm sorry," she said, looking directly at Joannie. "I'm so, so sorry."

"Thanks," Paula said.

Peter nodded. He crumpled his bag and got up to leave.

"See ya," was all Phil said. He left too.

When Mary Clare got up to leave she saw that Sister Agony was standing guard in the doorway. She held a broom in one hand and a dustpan in the other. Mary Clare could hear snickering at the hot lunch tables. The same kids who'd admired her yesterday for kicking that stone were laughing at her.

Sister leaned her head slightly to the left as Mary Clare took the broom from her. "Why aren't you eating hot lunch?" she asked. "Your family has always taken hot lunch. Your sisters just ate hot lunch."

"I just wanted a change," Mary Clare said. Here she was lying again. And her left pocket was already bulging with pebbles from so many sins. But nosey Sister Agony had left her no choice.

"Is that what your mother would say if I called and asked her?"

Mary Clare could feel the heat rising in her cheeks. Her eyes burned with unshed tears.

"Well?" Sister demanded.

Mary Clare was aware that the whole room was quiet. Everyone was waiting for her answer. She said nothing.

"I can go call your mother now."

"Don't," Mary Clare said. Hot tears tumbled down her cheeks in spite of her determination not to cry. "I was trying to save them some money."

"I'm sure," Sister said sarcastically. "Well, you've got some sweeping to do. You can use that big trash can there." She pointed to the dented aluminum one in the hall.

The first things that went into the trash can were the pebbles from her pocket. *It's too hard*, she thought. *Just too hard.*

Mary Clare O'Brian
188 Jackson Street
Littleburg, Wisconsin 53538

Sister Monica, Mother Superior
Saint Mary Magdalene Convent
1123 Good Shepherd Road
Minneapolis, Minnesota 55199

April 23, 1967

Dear Reverend Mother,

I am worried about whether or not it will be possible for me to become a Good Shepherd nun. Before I started paying attention to my sins I thought I was a pretty good person. I probably had a regular number of sins, but who knows, I never heard anybody else's confession. But when I decided to perfect myself the way the saints did and asked myself—Are you sure this isn't a sin, Mary Clare? Are you sure that's not a sin?—the sins started piling up like never before. Or at least I never realized how much I sin until now.

For example, Gabriella was prancing around in her First Communion dress—which was mine first and then Anne's, but it still looks great. She makes her First Confession on Friday and her First Communion is next Sunday. Anyway, she was being very vain, and I didn't want her to sin, so I told her Anne looked prettier in it. I had to count that as two sins because when I thought about it, what I said was mean and also not true, because Gabriella is every bit as cute as Anne. See what I mean?

I started using pebbles to keep perfect track of my sins, but I've given up because there were so many pebbles in my pocket by the end of the day, they were weighing me down and people were asking what made my pockets bulge.

Can you give me advice on how to stop sinning?

Sister Regina told us that saints had less than seven sins a day. How many sins can you have and still become a nun?

Please pray for me.

Sincerely,
Mary Clare

P.S. I think I'm beginning to understand what real humility is about.

7

The essay on religious vocations was due tomorrow. The essay that would win Mary Clare fifty dollars! If she won first place. If it was perfect. If it stood out, demanded attention, won the hearts of the judges. If it was the best of the best. That was why she had started it nineteen times and had a big fat nothing to show.

Everything she wrote was just plain ordinary. When she tried to dress it up, the words came out lacy. When she tried to be serious, the words came out prim and proper. When she tried to be funny, it sounded like she was making fun of vocations. And when she tried to compare nuns to priests, she sounded mad because she *was* mad. Priests got to say Mass, perform all the sacraments, touch the host ... and they could become pope. The closest nuns could get to the altar was to clean the sacristy and wash and iron the priest's vestments. They could never become cardinals or bishops or the pope.

Mary Clare reached for her last failed effort, which lay crumpled at the top of the waste basket. She smoothed it out and re-read it.

What does a vocation as a sister mean to me? Everything! Sisters are women who have devoted their lives to serving God through the vows of poverty, chastity, and obedience. Sisters devote their lives to prayer and doing God's work.

Yuck!

She leaned back in her father's swivel chair. He was presenting books in Chicago schools this week and his office was, by far, the safest part of the house to get work done—especially if she snuck in without anybody seeing her. She knew she needed to be quiet if she didn't want company, but she didn't want to be quiet. She wanted to scream! At this rate she'd be lucky to have something to turn in tomorrow, never mind an award-winning something.

Mary Clare could hear her mother hollering to the little kids to come inside for quiet hour, which her mother referred to as her "one salvation." Between 2:00 and 3:00 on weekend afternoons and every day in the summer, kids under the age of twelve had to be in their rooms napping or reading. During this time her mother could read or write or sew undisturbed. Mary Clare loved quiet hour, especially for her mother, who usually came out of her bedroom with more color in her face than before.

Mary Clare wanted to take a nap herself, or do anything but sit here writing an essay.

The door swung open and her mom stood in the doorway with a book in her hands, which she quickly tried to hide under her sweater. She didn't realize that Mary Clare had already seen the title.

"I wondered where you'd gone off to," her mother said.

Mary Clare started to gather her things together.

"Don't leave," her mother said. "I just want to sit in your father's easy chair for a while and read. Are you working on your essay?"

Mary Clare nodded and frowned.

"I'll take a peek at it if you'd like."

Mary Clare handed her the paragraph she'd retrieved from the trash. She watched as her mother read through it, then read through it a second time. She furrowed her eyebrows and looked up at Mary Clare.

"Don't just tell them what you think they want to hear, Mary Clare. Don't get into the roles everybody expects from a woman — where your identity is what the Church tells you it should be. 'God's servant, and God's bride' … that's just all part of the feminine mystique," she said. "Everybody knows what nuns *do* and the vows they take. Go inside your heart and tell them who you are."

Mary Clare was confused. She didn't know what the feminine mystique was, and she was pretty sure that to win this contest she had to pretty much say what the judges wanted to hear, but she *did* want to be real. She watched her mother cozy into the comfortable chair and open the book to a pen that was holding her place. She watched her mother read a little bit and then underline what she had read. Mary Clare couldn't help it.

"Why are you reading that Freidan book?" she asked. "You know Dad doesn't like 'women's libbers.'"

"I'm reading it because finally someone is acknowledging that being a housewife and mother are not going to fulfill every woman. Women need to get meaning through things other than their husbands and families. We need to use our minds, our creativity. We need to be more than baby machines."

Mary Clare thought about this. For some reason it made her squirm inside.

"Think about it! Women define themselves through men. If a man is successful, his wife gets to feel successful. If he's not, then she's not."

Mary Clare had never seen her mother this animated. She seemed like a different person. She wasn't sure about this new version of her mother.

"And the reason this book—this thinking—upsets your father so much is that he's scared he'll lose something if I look beyond him to be fulfilled."

"Oh," Mary Clare said. It was all she could think of to say. She understood her dad's fears more than her mother's new thinking. The idea of her mother finding fulfillment beyond the family scared her, too.

"The ironic thing about your father's reaction is that he hates censorship of any kind. But when it comes to feminist ideas, he'd love to keep me from thinking."

She paused and looked down at her watch. "We better stop talking or we'll miss the whole quiet hour."

Mary Clare sighed. She pulled out a fresh sheet of paper. She felt a little guilty doing the opposite of what her mother suggested, but she had an image in her head that would be a dramatic beginning. She asked God to inspire her.

WHAT A VOCATION AS A SISTER MEANS TO ME

I like to imagine walking down the aisle for my wedding. I'm wearing a white gown and a long lacy veil. My spouse waits for me at the altar. My spouse is Jesus. I am marrying him by answering his call to become a nun.

When Mary Clare completed her essay, the clock read 4:15. She couldn't be sure that it was a winner, but she'd certainly used her imagination in writing it. Behind her she saw her mother sleeping soundly. She crept out of the room, careful not to wake her, and tiptoed up the stairs to check on the little kids. The kids had already released themselves from their rooms, and she found them playing in the backyard. Mary Clare returned to her father's office and coaxed the book from her mother's hands without waking her. She had to see what the fuss was all about. She sat on the floor and began to read.

Mary Clare O'Brian
188 Jackson Street
Littleburg, Wisconsin 53538

Sister Monica, Mother Superior
Saint Mary Magdalene Convent
1123 Good Shepherd Road
Minneapolis, Minnesota 55199

May 1, 1967

Dear Reverend Mother,

I have a question about the women's liberation movement. Have you read Betty Friedan's book *The Feminine Mystique?* I tried to read it but it was too boring. My mom acts like it's a Bible. She has a whole bunch of corners turned down in it and she underlines things and puts exclamation marks in it. My parents fight about whether women should work or not and whether or not Mom should be happy as a housewife. Dad thinks Betty Friedan is out to destroy the family. Mom says Betty Friedan is just helping women wake up.

I just wondered if you read it and what you thought.

Sincerely,
Mary Clare

P.S. Why doesn't Saint Theresa the Little Flower stand up for herself instead of always turning the other cheek?

8

Mary Clare watched as her mother relit a half-smoked cigarette she had puffed on earlier that afternoon. She didn't need to ask her mother why she was smoking only partial cigarettes, then carefully putting them out and relighting them later. Dad got paid on the twenty-fifth of each month, and by the twentieth her parents were down to rationing their cigarettes.

This wasn't the way it was supposed to be. Not when she was trying so hard to be a saint. Yesterday she'd even given up her snack from the Camp Fire Girls meeting. It was a brownie. She'd brought it home and divided it between Margaret and Martha. If God wanted her to be a saint and make all these sacrifices, He was supposed to be making her mother and father happy and sending enough money so that they weren't struggling all the time.

It was true that her mother wasn't as depressed as before, but now she seemed angry. Angry and determined about something Mary Clare didn't really understand. And nothing had changed about money. Mary Clare paused. Maybe God didn't have faith in her. Maybe He thought she was too much of a sinner to become a saint.

Whatever God was thinking, Sister Charlotte said she would get the results of the essay contest by mid-May. Once she won, she'd know for sure that God wanted her to be a saint. Maybe they would get rich all at once. Mom would answer the phone cheerfully, instead of saying a quick Hail Mary that it wasn't a bill collector, and Dad would always have plenty of money in his pockets for meals out when he traveled.

Mary Clare gazed out the kitchen window at the red tulips that had opened overnight. She'd enjoyed the beautiful spring weather on the way home from school. The purple and white crocus had been out for weeks, but now the trees were budding, and her sisters were quick to point out each yard that boasted colorful tulips, grape hyacinth, or fragrant lilies of the valley. Summer was only weeks away and Mary Clare couldn't wait for the long days at Rock Lake. Most of her friends went to Lake Ripley, which was closer but cost money to get in. Rock Lake was free. And since she'd have to watch the kids anyway, it didn't much matter.

During her last class she had counted: only twenty-three days left of school for the year. Becky and Tina had twenty-four more days, because public school kids didn't get off school for Holy Days of Obligation. May 4 was a holy day, where Catholics were supposed to remember some mystery of the faith. Remembering meant not going to school and going to Mass instead.

When she'd gotten home, Mary Clare found her mother on the phone, her finger to her lips signaling everyone to be quiet. Mary Clare prompted the kids to go upstairs and change out of their uniforms. But she lingered behind to listen to her mother.

"Thank you," her mother was saying. "Then you'll send me an application in the mail?"

"An application for what?" Mary Clare asked when her mom got off the phone.

"None of your business," Mom said. But her voice was cheerful and her eyes flashed with excitement.

Mary Clare knew better than to press her mother, so she hurried up the stairs to get into a pair of jeans. She was in such a good mood that she decided to surprise her mother by cheerfully helping with dinner, cheerfully setting the table, and cheerfully doing the dishes, which might earn her saint points. Having now read *The Interior Castle*, she could see that Saint Theresa, the Little Flower, earned saint points by smiling and saying sweet things even when she was annoyed or in pain. Mary Clare might be floundering when it came to sins, but at least she could still do "good works."

When Mary Clare swung the closet door open to hang her uniform, she witnessed a miracle. There, in the back of the closet, a rosary glowed.

She gasped. Tears sprang to her eyes. This was a sign from God. He *did* want her to be a saint! He was going to accept her deal!

Suddenly the rosary started to jiggle. It swung wildly and finally dropped to the floor. She heard an unmistakable giggle. As her eyes adjusted to the light, she could make out a small body huddled against the back of the closet, reeling with laughter.

She had been had.

There was Gabriella—looking impish as she laughed, open-mouthed, revealing her chipped front tooth. Gabriella scrambled to pick up the rosary.

"Give me back my rosary, you little brat!" Mary Clare lunged at her sister, grabbing at the rosary in Gabriella's hand. Gabriella clutched it harder, still laughing until Mary Clare jerked it free and it flew across the room.

"You shouldn't have tried to trick me!" cried Mary Clare.

"I *did* trick you," said Gabriella. "You thought the rosary was a vision, didn't you?" She was wearing that snotty I'm-smarter-than-you-and-you're-nothing-but-a-fool look on her face that made Mary Clare want to slap her. "You're always looking for a miracle, Mary Clare."

Now Mary Clare wanted to tear the ribbons out of her sister's pigtails. Mary Clare turned away from her sister to collect herself. "Gabriella, you're so—cynical. You should believe in miracles."

Gabriella stood and picked up her rosary, now broken into three pieces. Her face twisted. "That was from Sister Lucy," she blubbered. Mary Clare knew that Gabriella loved her second grade teacher. She was young and bubbly, and whenever Mary Clare walked by the room the class seemed to be laughing.

Mary Clare was still furious, but she knew what she had to do. She went over to her bed and pulled out her own glow-in-the-dark rosary that lived under her pillow. "You can have this," she said, holding it out to Gabriella.

Gabriella's hands remained limp at her sides. "I don't want your dumb rosary. I want mine." She held out the broken one. "I'm going to take it to Sister Lucy and see if she can fix it."

"You can't call a rosary dumb! It's sacrilegious! These rosaries were blessed by the bishop."

Gabriella ignored her. "Maybe I'll get a new one for my First Communion anyway," she said.

Mary Clare didn't say a word. At the moment she didn't feel Gabriella deserved the First Communion things she'd worked so hard to get for her.

"I need your help with dinner, Mary Clare," her mother called from the bottom of the stairs.

"On my way," Mary Clare called. But as she was leaving the room, she spotted the First Confession booklet Gabriella had dropped on her bed.

"When's the important day?" Mary Clare tried to sound casual.

"What important day?"

"Your First Confession."

Gabriella shrugged. "Tomorrow."

"Have you thought about all your sins yet?"

Gabriella rolled her eyes. "I don't have any sins to confess."

"Of course you do!"

Gabriella looked big-eyed and innocent. "No, I don't."

Mary Clare could see that Gabriella wasn't playing. She really believed she was free from sin—like the Virgin Mary. Mary Clare took in a breath to give her patience.

"*Everybody* has sins, Gabriella. When you talk in class, or write notes in school, or gossip, or don't pay attention in church, those are all sins. Even saints sinned—of course they were only venial, and they kept them down to just a few a day, but they still had to go to confession. If you don't confess and do penance you're going to be in purgatory for a long, long time—or worse!"

Gabriella was focused on the Beatles poster that hung above Mary Clare's bed.

"Even the Beatles have sins on their souls," Mary Clare added.

"Except maybe for Paul," Gabriella said. She knew how much Mary Clare loved Paul.

"Mary Clare, get down here. I *need* you." Her mom's voice.

"In a minute!" Mary Clare snapped. It seemed far more important to straighten Gabriella out. "What about when you got caught stealing that gum from the 7–11 store? Stealing's a sin."

Gabriella's brown eyes sparkled and she tossed her braids impishly. "That was before Christmas and I was only six. It doesn't count."

She had a point, of course. A kid could murder somebody at six and it wouldn't count. Her soul would remain lily white. But turn seven, and everything counted. Big ugly blotches of darkness stained the soul with every infraction.

"Okay," Mary Clare said. "But you've been seven for three months. You have to have tons of sins by now."

Mary Clare picked up the First Confession booklet on Gabriella's bed and leafed through it, looking for the page listing all the sins.

"That's mine!" Gabriella objected.

Mary Clare was puzzled. How could anybody prepare for confession unless they had a list of sins? She picked up her own missal that lay on top of her books. It was her First Communion missal, white with a gold cross embossed on top. She flipped to the section on confession and opened to the tattered page that contained all the sins a person read through when they examined their conscience in preparation for each confession. She brought them over to Gabriella, who studied them seriously for a time and then burst out laughing.

"Lust, coveting your neighbor's wife, the seven deadly sins—this is all so old-fashioned. Sister Lucy says that God is love and He loves us no matter what."

Mary Clare seethed as she thought about the pebbles she'd tried using to track every little sin, and here was Gabriella thinking she had no sins at all.

"But look *here*," Mary Clare said, pointing to the next column. "Lying, answering back to your parents, fighting with your brothers and sisters . . . You commit those sins all the time."

Gabriella held the missal but turned her face away from the words so she didn't have to look.

Mary Clare jerked it out of Gabriella's hands. "You are *not* ready to make your First Confession, Gabriella."

Gabriella's face scrunched up. The light in her eyes dimmed, then filled with tears. "Sister says I'm ready. And you're just mean."

"MARY CLARE! If I have to come up there . . ."

Mary Clare bolted from the bed. "Coming!"

"Gee," Gabriella called after her. "I think you've been *disobedient*. Isn't that a *sin*?"

The dishes seemed to slam down on the table of their own accord as Mary Clare set it for dinner. How could Gabriella not even realize that she had sins to confess? It wasn't right. Maybe Sister Lucy wasn't teaching them the right things about confession.

"What has gotten into you, Mary Clare?" asked her mother. "If those dishes weren't Melmac they'd all be shattered. Come in here and wash up the lettuce. I'll have Gabriella finish setting the table." Her mother went to the staircase and told Gabriella to come downstairs.

Gabriella meandered down the stairs wearing jeans, a tee shirt, and a scowl.

"Why me?" Gabriella argued when her mother told her to set the table. "Why can't Anne do it?"

"Because Anne is taking care of Johnny."

"Margaret could . . ."

"Gabriella. Enough! Finish setting the table," their mother said.

Mary Clare wouldn't let herself look at her little sister. She would have glared and that would have been another sin. Instead she focused on the carrots and potatoes she was washing.

Gabriella pulled a stack of glasses out of the cabinet and brought them to the dining room table. "Anybody eating over tonight?" she asked. She was counting the glasses.

"Not that I know of," their mother said.

"I wish everything matched," Gabriella said. "At Sarah's house the glasses match the plates and bowls and everything. The salt and pepper shakers even match the dishes."

"Sarah's an only child," Mary Clare said.

"I know," Gabriella said. "I wish I were an . . ."

Their mom stopped cutting the potatoes. Stopped cold.

Now Mary Clare did give her sister a dirty look. She could tell by how Gabriella was looking at their mom that she knew she had made a mistake.

Their mother resumed cutting potatoes, but she cut slowly and deliberately. She didn't turn to look at either daughter, and the girls continued their tasks in silence.

Finally their mother sped up her cutting again and the girls knew that she was okay. "I think someday you may appreciate having brothers and sisters," she said.

"I already do, sometimes," Gabriella said.

When their mother opened the oven to check on the chicken, the smell wafted through the room and made Mary Clare realize that she was hungry. She could hear the living room door open and the familiar voices of Mark and his friend Flipper chatting. They came right to the kitchen.

"Dinner sure smells good, Mrs. O'Brian," Flipper said. It was his typical hint to get himself invited to dinner, which he did three or four times a week. He flashed a half smile toward Mary Clare's mom and winked at Mary Clare while he chewed his Wrigley spearmint gum. Flipper always chewed Wrigley spearmint gum.

"You'll just have to stay and see if it tastes as good as it smells," Mom said.

"Thanks, Mrs. O'Brian. I will."

Mary Clare took out another place setting and handed it to Gabriella. She loved it when Flipper stayed. He was so cute. He was tall with dishwater-blonde hair that fell to his shoulders, and he treated Mary Clare as if she were a high school kid.

"We'll be eating in twenty minutes," their mom called after Mark and Flipper. They were already heading up the stairs to Mark's room.

It was a typical weekday dinner, with their father on the road and Matthew at the seminary. Luke made it home just as they were about to sit down to the table. He was excited about another folk song he'd just learned on his guitar and hinted that he might play it for the family later.

After dinner they all brought their own plates to the kitchen. Mary Clare used a spatula to scrape the leftover food into a colander and handed them, one by one, to Flipper, who insisted on washing the dishes. It always irritated Mark how Flipper did this, but it thrilled Mary Clare. Their mom handed towels to Anne and Gabriella and a soapy dish rag to Mark so he could wash off the table and counters. Mary Clare rolled the garbage in old newspaper. Luke was supposed to take it out to the garbage cans, but he'd disappeared.

Just as the cleanup was almost finished, the sound of Luke's guitar summoned everyone to the living room, where he had positioned himself in an armchair and was playing a Bob Dylan song he had just learned. Even Flipper and Mark stuck around to hear it. When he had finished, Anne made the first request for songs the whole family knew. "Sing 'Puff the Magic Dragon,'" she begged.

"No, sing some Beatles songs," Gabriella insisted. She started humming one: "If I fell in love with you, would you promise to be true?"

"Hey, I didn't agree to play any more," Luke said, but he started strumming the tune to a Beatles song, and soon even little Johnny was dancing and clapping to the music.

It was amazing, the power that music held to bring them together, Mary Clare thought. It was practically a miracle. The kids could be fighting, her parents could be bickering, they could be squished together in the car, but music worked magic in bringing them together. It was an everyday miracle that was part of their lives long before Mary Clare asked for a miracle. And it made her grateful every time.

Luke played a mixture of folk music and rock and roll—everything from Woody Guthrie's "This Land is My Land" to Gladys Knight and the Pips. Luke ended with one of Mary Clare's favorites, "Where Have All the Flowers Gone?"

By the time the singing was over, Mary Clare helped her mother lay out clothes for the little kids for school the next day. While Mom checked to make sure the uniform pieces were all clean and pressed, Mary Clare laid out underwear and socks. By the time she made it to the television, where the rest of the family sat, the closing credits were already flashing across the screen.

"Turn off the television, Anne. It's time for you girls to start getting ready for bed," Mom said.

As Anne reluctantly walked over to the television and switched it off, Mary Clare noticed that Margaret was slicking Johnny's hair back with a huge gob of Dippity-do, the sticky, icky hair-styling gel.

"Mom!" Mary Clare cried.

Everyone looked over at Margaret and Johnny.

"It looks nice!" Margaret insisted, placing her hands on her hips. Johnny just laughed.

Chaos ensued: Whose was it? Where'd she get it from? Who was going to wash Johnny's hair and get him into his pajamas?

"This is my whole life!" their mother said. "Cleaning up messes, taking care of everyone's needs. I swear, being a mother saps any kind of intelligence or creativity right out of a person." She began to cry. Mary Clare sighed. It was that Betty Friedan stuff again, making her mother so miserable.

Finally it was sorted out. Mary Clare admitted she'd bought the Dippity-do ages ago to help straighten her hair, and she agreed to put it someplace where the little kids wouldn't get into it and to never bring anything into the house secretly again. Anne volunteered to put Johnny in his pajamas after Mom said she'd wash his hair in the morning.

When she returned from the bathroom, where she had placed the jar on the highest shelf in the medicine cabinet, Gabriella was talking to their mother.

"I need a new pair of shoes for my First Communion," Gabriella was saying. Mary Clare sighed. How could Gabriella be that oblivious to the family's financial struggles?

"What about the shoes Mary Clare and Anne wore for their First Communion?" her mother asked.

"Those pinch my toes. Besides, I should have something new. I'm wearing a hand-me-down dress, a hand-me-down veil, even a hand-me-down *slip*."

Mary Clare looked at her mother's face. Her eyes were fogged over like they were looking at something far, far away. But Gabriella seemed oblivious. She kept right on going.

"Everybody else has something new. I want . . ."

Mother raised her hand in a "stop" motion. "Tomorrow. We'll talk about it tomorrow."

That night, when Mary Clare went to bed, she had to say two entire rosaries to stop thinking mean thoughts about her sister.

Saint Mary Magdalene Convent and School
1123 Good Shepherd Road
Minneapolis, Minnesota 55199

Mary Clare O'Brian
189 Jackson St.
Littleburg, Wisconsin 53538

May, 1967

Dear Mary Clare,

When I received your last letter, I was surprised, pleased, and somewhat concerned over how distressed you've become over your sins. I was surprised because it seems like such a change from the confident person you were in your first letter. I was pleased because it tells me how serious you are about pleasing God and becoming a nun. And I was concerned because you are making your life more anxious than it needs to be.

Remember that St. Theresa's confessor told her she needed to stop being so scrupulous about her sins. If you worry about every little thing, it will make you crazy. I can't imagine God wanting any of His children to go crazy. God is love, and that means that when God looks at you, He sees all that you do through loving eyes. When you examine your conscience before bed, try looking at yourself and everyone else through God's loving eyes.

Being too scrupulous about your sins is itself a sin. If you're that caught up in every little thing you say or do, you are forgetting that God is love and that He is forgiving. Instead, ask yourself the bigger questions: Am I a loving person? Am I kind? Am I generous?

I am so happy that Pope John XXIII helped the Church refocus on love instead of fear. Think of how much joy you will experience in your life when you stop thinking so much about sin and place your attention on being loving the way Jesus was!

Of course I'll pray for you. I pray for you every day.

God bless you!
Mother Monica

9

Mary Clare noticed that Sister Charlotte wasn't at Mass on Wednesday morning. She usually sat in the nineteenth pew, directly behind the sixth grade class. She wasn't out in front of the school where everyone gathered after Mass to say the Pledge of Allegiance, or anywhere in sight when the first bell rang. When the class filed into the room and took their seats, Sister Charlotte was still not there, and when the second bell rang, signaling the start of religion class, Tommy decided the class should give Sister a detention slip for being tardy. Gregory offered to take one from her desk and hand it to her when she came in.

Finally Sister appeared in the doorway, looking very different from the way she usually did.

"Wow!" Phil said when Sister appeared.

"Look!" Jen said.

"Sister!" the DeLuca twins said.

Mary Clare's mouth fell open. She couldn't think of anything to say.

"This is the new habit of the Sisters of St. Francis," Sister said. She held her hands out so everyone could appreciate her new look. Her face was as red as an apple with so many eyes scrutinizing her.

Suddenly the whole class was on their feet, clapping and cheering and all talking at once.

"Please take your seats," Sister said, laughing. "Then I'll answer all your questions." She moved some papers off the corner of her desk and sat on top of it, facing the class.

The new habit was an abbreviation of the old one. Unlike the old veil that hung midway down her back, this one only came to her shoulders and didn't completely cover her hair. The girls, who had long speculated as to the color of Sister's hair, could now see wisps of brown waves exposed under the veil. Instead of a wimple covering her neck, the new habit sported a white Peter Pan collar. Her neck was bare. Instead of the all-enveloping full-length sleeves in which the nuns hid handkerchiefs and God only knew what else, the new sleeves were three-quarter length with turned-up cuffs. She wore a black bolero-style jacket over a dress of the same fabric. Her dress fell just below her knees, revealing black tights and sensible black shoes. Mary Clare thought that Sister Charlotte looked completely modern—and even cuter than before.

The questions were coming at Sister hard and fast.

"No." Sister said. Not all the other nuns were wearing the new habit. Only she and Sister Lucy had accepted the trial.

"Yes." Sister said. The new design was directly related to Vatican II. Pope John, she said, thought that nuns should wear habits that were practical for the work they were doing. "The thing I like best about the new habit is that it's so freeing," she added. "The old habit weighed at least twice this much."

Before Sister Charlotte finished the sentence, several students were standing in response to the sudden appearance of Sister Agony at the door. Sister Charlotte slid off the desk to a standing position. Her face looked like an apple all over again.

"Good morning, Sister Agnes," the class recited in unison.

For a split second Sister Agony's eyes narrowed as she took in Sister Charlotte's new habit. Sister Charlotte diverted her eyes as if she were embarrassed. The air was thick with tension between the two nuns, giving Mary Clare a queasy feeling in her stomach. She had never considered that nuns might disagree or actually argue over anything. But from the looks of it, she had been mistaken.

"I'm sorry to disturb your religion class," Sister Agony said, not looking at all as if she were sorry. "But this is important." She looked down at the envelope she held in her hand.

"Certainly," Sister Charlotte said. She stepped away from the desk and leaned against the chalkboard behind her. Mary Clare looked from Sister Agony to Sister Charlotte, taking in the contrast in habits. The old habit that had always been normal now seemed excessive — too much fabric, the wimple too stiff and confining around the face, too old-fashioned. Sister Agony gave the class a rare smile. "I just received a letter from the diocese regarding the Vocational Essay Contest you all entered." Sister Charlotte's mouth fell open. She stood up straighter and approached Sister Agony, peering at the envelope Sister Agony held.

"It's good news, I assure you," Sister Agony said to the class.

Mary Clare forgot to breathe. She could feel several sets of eyes peering at her. And she was sure others were peering at Gregory. Finally, finally, finally she would get her sign from God. If she won, God would be telling her that she was meant to be a saint, and that He was going to help her family.

"Let me read the letter to you," Sister Agony said. Mary Clare crossed her fingers. Then she uncrossed them. This was not about luck. It was about God.

" 'Dear Sister Charlotte,' " Sister Agony began. She paused and glanced at Sister Charlotte's face.

Mary Clare took in a sharp breath as she watched Sister Charlotte bite her lip. The letter was addressed to *her*. It was Sister Charlotte who had submitted their essays. Why was Sister Agony opening and reading Sister Charlotte's mail? Was she just trying to show Sister that she had more power?

"'We received wonderful responses for the Vocational Essay Contest from 564 very talented sixth graders throughout the Madison diocese. The writing was so good, and the sentiments so dear, that the judges found it impossible to narrow the search to first, second, and third place winners.'"

Mary Clare felt her fingers curl into fists. It wasn't fair. The rest of the letter sounded like it was coming through a long tunnel. She had trouble making sense of the words and their meaning.

"'The judges have narrowed the number of potential winners to ten. We are asking the ten finalists to enter a one-page addendum from which we will select the three winners. I have attached a separate page concerning the content we are looking for in the addendum.

"'Congratulations to St. Maria Goretti School in Littleburg, Wisconsin, for the distinction of being the only school to have two contest finalists: Gregory Kowalski and Mary Clare O'Brian.'"

The class clapped politely. She couldn't make herself look directly at Gregory, but from the corner of her eye she could see that he was looking at her.

Sister continued the letter. "'In consideration of the fact that this is the end of the school year, the finalists will not be required to turn in their addendums until September thirty. We realize that all our candidates will be in the seventh grade at that time. We apologize for any inconvenience this delay may cause, but we sincerely hope that our candidates will accept the challenge to submit the addendum. All finalists who submit an addendum will receive a minimum of ten dollars award money.'"

Sister Agony released the letter and papers to Sister Charlotte, who responded with a curt nod.

"Congratulations, Gregory and Mary Clare," Sister Agony said, smiling in the general direction of each of them. She turned and walked out of the classroom.

"Yes," Sister Charlotte said. Her face was still splotchy red and her lips were thin, but she offered Mary Clare and Gregory a wide smile. "I'm proud of both of you."

The discussion of Sister Charlotte's new habit and Sister Agony's letter had taken the entire religion class. When the bell rang and students remembered the upcoming history test, there were more than a few moans.

Mary Clare was one of the moaners. She couldn't imagine how she could possibly concentrate on a history test. She was still trying to digest the letter. It was such a disappointment that the judges hadn't picked out a winner outright. *What does this mean, God? Are you testing me, putting me in the top ten but not letting me win? Is it that you want me to work harder at being a saint?* She was so frustrated she wanted to scream, but everyone seemed to think she should be happy with the results. *I think I know what you're doing, God. You're trying to make me humble, aren't you?* And what was it supposed to mean that Gregory Kowalski, of all people, was one of her competitors?

Mary Clare and Sister Charlotte shared a private smile when Sister handed her the history test. Sister's smile was probably meant to congratulate her, but Mary Clare's smile was meant to comfort Sister Charlotte, to say she understood that Sister Agony had hurt her. Mary Clare reminded herself how lucky she was to have Sister Charlotte all day and not have to rotate classrooms and teachers like the public school kids had to. She got the best teacher in the world from morning through last period. She pulled out a pencil, wrote "JMJ" on the top, as usual, for Jesus, Mary, and Joseph, and tried to concentrate.

Sister Charlotte began her rhythmic walk between the aisles, checking on the progress of each student and looking, no doubt, for cheaters. She would give time reports as she walked: "Fifteen more minutes, ten more minutes." When she paused in front of Mary Clare she smelled like Ivory soap and peppermint. "Five more minutes," she said, wrinkling her forehead as she examined Mary Clare's paper. Mary Clare had two essay questions she hadn't even started on. Sister locked her hands behind her back and continued patrolling the classroom.

"Anyone who needs extra time on the test can stay in during recess to finish," Sister said. It was a rare and generous concession. Mary Clare, who had almost written the test off for lack of concentration, began to tackle the questions in earnest. When the bell rang she hardly noticed students handing in their papers or the inevitable noise in the hallway as they rushed to get outside. Only when she completed the last sentence of the last essay question did she notice that she and Gregory were the only two people left in the classroom. Apparently he hadn't been able to concentrate any better than she had.

Gregory beat her to the front of the classroom, where he placed his paper on the top of the stack and waited awkwardly for Mary Clare to hand hers in.

Sister handed each of them the sheets that described the addendum they were to write. They read silently.

Vocation Essay Addendum Guidelines
Finalists should submit a one-page, double-spaced paper that includes but is not limited to the following: their personal prayer life and that of Religious, the meaning of the vows they take as well as the sacrament men receive when they become priests. They should include something

102

about the service they see themselves providing in the order they are considering.

The original prize structure will remain in effect: fifty dollars for first prize, thirty for second prize, and fifteen for third prize. We hope all the finalists will continue in the contest by submitting an addendum in September.

Gregory grinned. "Congratulations," he said as they walked into the hallway.

"Congratulations back," Mary Clare said. Just as Mary Clare was about to make an excuse and race ahead, Gregory touched her arm. "How come you wouldn't look at me before?"

"When?" she asked.

"Before—when Sister announced we were in the top ten."

Mary Clare shrugged. "I was just surprised."

"Surprised that I was in the top ten? Or surprised that you didn't win outright?"

"Both," Mary Clare blurted.

Gregory burst into laughter when Mary Clare grimaced at her own mistake. "That's what I like about you, Mary Clare. You don't pretend to be modest about your talent."

Mary Clare glared at Gregory. "I can be modest!"

Gregory roared with laughter. "You can be, but it sure doesn't come natural."

"It's just—I didn't know you were so religious!" she said.

"Maybe I'm not," he said. "Maybe I just know how to sound religious in an essay."

Mary Clare glared at him. She raced ahead to the girls' bathroom, where he couldn't disturb her and where she could consider the delicious possibility that if Gregory wasn't religious, maybe he still liked her.

Mary Clare O'Brian
188 Jackson Street
Littleburg, Wisconsin 53538

Sister Monica, Mother Superior
Saint Mary Magdalene Convent
1123 Good Shepherd Road
Minneapolis, Minnesota 55199

May 9, 1967

Dear Reverend Mother,

Your last letter gave me the answer that I was looking for in one of
my first letters—whether or not you were an old-fashioned nun or
a modern-day nun. You are definitely modern-day! I feel a lot better
not focusing on sins so much.

　　Is your convent getting new habits? Two of our nuns, out of
seven, have new habits they're trying out. Sister Charlotte said that
Franciscan nuns may eventually do away with habits altogether. I
hope not. How would nuns get the respect they deserve without the
habit? I hope the Good Shepherd nuns don't make too many habit
changes.

　　　　　　　　　　　　　　　　Sincerely,
　　　　　　　　　　　　　　　　Mary Clare

P.S. I have a question. Why is the Virgin Mary always crying?
Whenever I close my eyes to say a prayer, I see an image of her
crying. It makes me feel guilty, like I've done something wrong.

10

●●●

"Matthew's coming home this weekend," Mary Clare's mom announced the next evening.

Mary Clare let the baby bottle slip into the dishwater. It smacked on the bottom of the sink.

"Be careful. If you break one of those you'll cut your hand on the glass."

Mary Clare tried to sound casual. "Will the band be practicing here this weekend?" She picked up another bottle.

Her mother let out a sigh. "Where else? They've got a 'gig' in Watertown Saturday night, so they'll practice on Friday. I told them it's the garage or nothing. And they have to quit before ten o'clock. I don't want the neighbors complaining."

Mary Clare picked up the bottle brush and was careful not to drop any more bottles. She smiled as she thought of the plan she and Joannie had thought up: the next time Matthew was home from the seminary they would ask him if he and his band, The Seminarians, would play for a party. Her party! No one in her class or her whole school had ever given a party with a live band. It would be so wonderful. And most importantly, it would bring her back into the popular group. Everyone would be dying to get invited to a party with a live band.

Things had gone from bad to worse since she ate cold lunch with the unpopular kids and admitted to Sister Agony that she was trying to save her parents' money. When she told Jen that she loved her new spring coat and asked where she had gotten it, Jen had turned away at first, then turned back and said, "It doesn't matter, Mary Clare. I don't think your family could afford a coat like this." She'd said it right in front of everybody.

It wasn't even clear anymore that Kelly was still her best friend. She was still nice enough to Mary Clare, but she seemed more interested in being with Sandra and Jen and the rest of the group.

But meanwhile Mary Clare and Joannie were getting to be better friends, and it was Joannie who had agreed to help Mary Clare plan the party.

They planned how to warm up Matthew to the idea. They'd wait until he was in a good mood—when he was listening to music in his room. They'd tell him how good his band had gotten. Then they'd tell him how much their friends would love to hear them. Mary Clare would even offer to do Matthew's laundry for a whole month if he said yes. Once Matthew was sold, he'd ask the rest of the band, Butch, Carl, and Dennis, all seniors in high school just like Matthew. And after *they'd* said yes, she would talk Mom into it. Then they'd pray that Mom would get an okay from Dad ... which would probably be fine. Even though Dad and Matthew fought constantly, Dad enjoyed the band a lot.

"You're dreaming again, Mary Clare," her mother said. She nodded her head toward the stove so Mary Clare would see that the bottle sterilizer was already heating up with three empty slots waiting for the bottles she had yet to wash. It was a job Mary Clare and her mother did every two days. The bottles, nipples, and screw tops had to be boiled for fifteen to twenty minutes, and after they had cooled down they'd fill each with formula and refrigerate them. Mary Clare liked the feeling of having sixteen full bottles. Then when the babies cried, she'd only have to warm them up under the faucet for a few minutes. Mary Clare dunked the last baby bottle into the warm water and brushed it clean.

"Done!" she proclaimed, handing it to her mother.

"Would you please ..." Mom stopped, because Mary Clare had already grabbed the broom and started sweeping.

"Thank you, honey. You're a saint. I don't know what I'd do without you."

Mary Clare smiled. She imagined the promises she'd make to her mother if she agreed to the party. "I'll clean the whole house from top to bottom if you say yes," she'd say, and her mother would say again, "You are a saint."

Mary Clare plopped down on the couch between Gabby and the little kids and pretended to watch *Gunsmoke*. Instead she prayed. *Please, God, I really want to have this party. You probably don't think I should care about popularity, but think of how many souls I could save if people really liked me. I still want to be a saint, God. So I need a sign, something that makes it clear that it's okay to have a party.* She sighed, thinking about how she had just prayed a selfish prayer, and how Saint Monica was selfless as she prayed incessantly for her son to convert. Mary Clare quickly prayed six Hail Mary's and an Our Father. She made a mental note to pray for the unpopular kids and pagan babies the next day in Mass. *But still,* she continued bargaining with God. *If Matthew says yes to the party, I'll take that as a yes from You. If he says no, I'll take that as a no from You.*

On Friday, Mary Clare looked forward to seeing Matthew all day. She invited Joannie over for dinner so they could talk to Matthew together. But when the family sat down to goulash, green beans, homemade dinner rolls, and salad, Matthew wasn't there yet and Mary Clare was nervous because her father was. Normally she avoided having friends over when her father was home on the weekends. He might be in a great mood one minute, furious the next. And he didn't really care about who was listening. Things could get especially tense if he and Matthew started fighting again.

Mary Clare looked around. Her father, at the head of the table, was heaping the goulash onto his plate and talking about his work in Chicago over the last week. He seemed to be in a mood. Mom was nodding toward Dad to show she was listening, but Mary Clare could see she had other things on her mind. Four of the younger kids were crowded onto the window seat, which spanned one side of the table. The older boys, Mark and Luke, were sitting on the opposite side of the table at the end near their dad. Then came Joannie, Mary Clare, Johnny in his high chair, and Mom at the opposite end. So far there were no spills or tears, and only two or three conversations at once.

When Dad took a bite of goulash, Mark broke into the conversation.

"Dad, I want to tell you something," he said. Everyone stopped. His voice sounded urgent.

"Go ahead," Dad said as soon as he had swallowed.

"Flipper joined the army today."

"He's too young!" The response was a chorus from both ends of the table.

Mary Clare heard the front door close and peeked into the living room, where Matthew was dragging his laundry bag across the floor.

"Who's too young?" Matthew asked. He leaned his laundry bag against the dining room wall and began looking around for a chair to join the family at the table. A chorus of voices tried to answer him at the same time.

"Flipper? You're kidding. He's just sixteen!" Matthew said.

"Yup," Mark said. "His dad signed the papers."

Martha crawled under the table to get to Matthew. When she hugged his leg she left a tomatoey mess on his pants, but Mary Clare seemed to be the only one who noticed.

"He's gonna get himself killed," Dad said.

"And for a war we shouldn't even be fighting," Matthew added. His voice trailed as he left the dining room and walked into the kitchen.

Dad dropped his fork and pointed a finger at Matthew. "I won't have this kind of talk in my house," he thundered.

"Dad, even nuns and priests are protesting this war," Matthew said.

"Now wait, I've certainly heard of priests fighting for civil rights—Father Groppi in Milwaukee, for instance—but I haven't heard of any priest protesting the war," Dad said.

"Well, I'm the one in the seminary and I know priests who do."

Mary Clare's body tensed. She looked at Joannie's frozen face. Her eyes had grown big and she was focused on the salt shaker in the middle of the table. One by one Anne, Gabriella, and Margaret asked to be excused and left the table.

Good thinking. Mary Clare wished she could do the same, but her plate was still loaded with food because she'd been spoon-feeding Johnny.

"Come on, Dad, don't yell," Mark said. "I need to talk to you about this."

Matthew returned to the table, plate and silverware in hand. He scrunched behind the table, where there was now plenty of room at the window seat.

"What was he thinking?" Dad asked. "Why would his parents agree to this?"

Matthew said nothing. But he slammed the serving spoons

against his plate as he was loading it with food and held his silverware in his fist.

"For one thing he's sick and tired of being suspended for no good reason," Mark said. "Like this morning, he got suspended for not tucking in his shirt—not tucking in his shirt, for crying out loud! So we decided to go up to Madison and see a recruitment officer."

"Wait a minute, you ditched school?" Dad said.

Joannie was pushing food around her plate with her fork but nothing made it to her mouth. Mary Clare bit her bottom lip. She knew she should get Joannie out of here, but she was glued to her chair.

"Not exactly," Mark said, running his finger along the outside of his metal tumbler.

Mom let out a long, exhausted breath. "Mark was also suspended." She let her fork slip out of her hand as if she were simply too tired to eat. "For not wearing a belt." You had to listen hard to make out her words.

"You *knew* about this?" Dad hollered.

All eyes were now on Mom. All except for Joannie, who looked like she might start to cry. Mary Clare thought she should excuse herself and get Joannie out of there, but she was too interested in seeing who Dad would be madder at—Mark for getting suspended, Mom for not telling him right away, or Mr. Mooney, the high school principal, for giving him a suspension.

As the children watched silently, Dad's anger swung between "the asininity of the school for its shirttail and belt policies" and "the sheer audacity of Mark going to Madison in Flipper's dilapidated VW Beetle without permission."

"Paul," Mom said, her voice cajoling. "You just got home from five days on the road. Why don't you relax? Deal with this tomorrow when you've had a little rest."

"Rest!" Dad said. "The only rest I get is when I'm in a motel at night."

"That's fine—that's so nice for you, Paul." Mom's voice was quiet steel. Her eyes were fire, and the flames were directed at Dad. "You get rest in your fancy hotel rooms and peace and quiet when you're flying or driving. Meanwhile I'm home taking care of nine children and another on the way. I don't get peace and quiet. I don't get a break from responsibility. Then you come home and I have to worry about you too."

Mom stood up and stormed out of the room, leaving Dad silent, still scowling.

Mary Clare watched her mother ascend the stairs, stunned at her anger. She looked at Joannie, who was sitting up so straight and stiff she looked like she had a pole in her back. Johnny whined and held his arms out to Mary Clare. She lifted him out of the high chair. Martha looked like she would start wailing any second but Anne got to her first. She hugged Martha and told her not to worry, everything was fine.

"Wait!" Mark said finally. "I was trying to make a point." Everyone paused and looked at him. Mark turned to face his father. "I'm sorry I went to Madison without permission. But I wanted to find out about the army as badly as Flipper did. I learned a lot today, and I decided that I want to enlist too."

Mary Clare had never seen her father's eyes open as wide as they were at that moment.

"I filled out the paperwork. All I need is your signature."

"No!" Matthew said, looking at Dad. "You can't let him!"

Dad didn't respond to Mark or Matthew. His focus was somewhere far away.

Mary Clare stood up and motioned to Joannie to follow. It was clear that things weren't going to get better any time soon. The two were almost to the front door when Matthew called her name.

"Yeah?" She hesitated, watching as Joannie bolted out the front door and ran across the street toward her house. Mary Clare didn't blame her for wanting to get away, but … She returned to the dining room, where Dad and Mark were still yelling at each other.

"What did you want, Matthew?" Mary Clare asked when she could get a word in.

"I just wanted to hear your opinion. Do you think Mark should go to Vietnam? I mean, what do you think about the war?"

"Who cares what she thinks?" Mark said. "I'm trying to get *Dad's* opinion."

Mary Clare felt her throat tighten. Matthew was really putting her on the spot. "I think …" she began. She stopped. It occurred to her that whatever she said would offend someone.

"What do you think?" Dad asked, suddenly looking curious.

Three sets of eyes were focused on Mary Clare. She was frozen in place. War and politics were stuff the guys talked about. Matthew had talked to her a few times about marching for civil rights, and she'd loved it because it made her feel like an adult. But she wasn't even sure she had an opinion on Vietnam. "I, I think …" Mary Clare looked at her father. She didn't want him to be angry at her too. She looked at Matthew, whose face showed the kind of respect she had always wanted from him. But she didn't know if the war was right or wrong. She didn't know if Matthew was right to refuse to fight or if Mark was right to want to go. "I don't know," she said. She raced through the living room and out the door, hearing Mark snicker behind her.

"I told you she didn't know," he said.

Mary Clare saw Joannie sitting on her front porch, but she just kept running. She ran down the hill past the Henderson house, the Turners', the Andersons', past the Stop and Go. She ran across Madison Avenue and kept running all the way to Mercer Park. There she slowed down to catch her breath. Her lungs felt ready to burst, but they didn't hurt as much as the humiliation. She was tempted to sit on one of the swings but it was getting dark, so she forced herself to turn around and begin the mile-long hike back.

She tried to picture Mark and Flipper in army uniforms but the image seemed ridiculous. Both sported long haircuts, and when they weren't dressed nicely for school they wore tie-dyed tee shirts and raggedy jeans. She tried to remember clips she'd seen on the news arguing about the war. She wished she had paid more attention. What she had paid attention to were the terrible images she'd seen on television—whole villages on fire, landmines exploding, people screaming, reports of hundreds of soldiers killed or captured every week. And then there were all the protests right here in the United States. Hundreds— maybe thousands of people in the street holding up signs that said things like "Make Love Not War" and "Question Authority." Young men burning draft cards.

As she reached Madison Avenue, it occurred to Mary Clare that she didn't need to know all the arguments for or against American involvement to know that she opposed war, any war.

When she came within three houses from hers, she knew the fighting wasn't over, and apparently so did the rest of the neighborhood. She glanced furtively toward the Henderson house, next to theirs, and was relieved to see that the lights weren't on and there was no car in the driveway. The Marino family was clearly home. The lights were all on. She hoped they had the television on loud or were listening to music. She hoped that Joannie hadn't told them about the fight.

Joannie answered the door after the first knock.

"I'm sorry," she and Joannie said at the exact same time.

"It's just that your family's so ..."

"Loud," Mary Clare finished.

"Well, yeah," Joannie admitted. "Do you want to come in?"

"No, thank you. I just wanted to make sure you were all right. I never should have invited you for dinner when Dad and Matthew were home at the same time."

Joannie nodded. "I'm sorry I won't be able to help you talk to Matthew."

Mary Clare had actually forgotten about the party. She'd been too wrapped up in the discussion of war, and how Joannie was faring through it all.

"Gosh, Joannie, maybe my family's too messed up for me to have a party."

Joannie contemplated this for a minute. "I bet your family will act better during a party," she said.

"I suppose," Mary Clare said. But she couldn't be sure.

Matthew was still talking when Mary Clare returned home a few minutes later. "This war is wrong. And I'm not going. I'm not going to kill another man and I won't put myself in a position to be killed."

"What, you're going to burn your draft card when you get it and wind up arrested like that, that kid ...?"

"James Wilson," Matthew said. "Yeah, maybe."

"If your country needs you to fight, you will," Dad said. "I fought in World War Two and your grandfather fought in World War One. It's the way it's always been. When your country needs you, you fight." Dad punctuated each word with his fist on the table.

Matthew, Mark, and Luke were still at the table. Everybody else had taken off.

Mary Clare slowly cleared the table. That way she had an excuse to be in the room and hear what was going on.

Mark and Matthew were talking at the same time. Mark won out because he was louder.

"Dad, I *want* to fight for my country. You're telling Matthew he has to fight if he gets drafted, but then you refuse to sign for me so I *can* fight for my country. I don't get it."

Yeah, that was what Mary Clare didn't get either.

"You'll finish high school first. And that's final," Dad said. He stood up, threw his napkin on his plate, and pointed at Matthew. "And you! You *will* serve your country if you're drafted. You will not become a conscientious objector. I won't have a coward for a son." He climbed the first couple of stairs but paused when he saw Mom at the top.

"Sit down, Paul. We've all just got to calm down about this." It was strange to Mary Clare to hear her mother take charge like this. Stranger still was the fact that Dad only hesitated for a second before doing as she said. Mary Clare couldn't be sure if it was shock or respect that made him listen.

For the next few minutes the only sound in the room was that of Mary Clare scraping the remains of one plate onto another so she could stack them in the sink. She could hear Mom in the kitchen filling the coffee pot with water. She glanced at the faces of each remaining person in the room. Dad's forehead was furrowed, and he rubbed his chin with his thumb and forefinger just like he always did when he was deep in thought. Mark fumed. But it was Matthew's face, scrunched up like he was going to cry, that filled her chest with heaviness.

Mary Clare's eyes blurred with tears. *How could Dad call him a coward?* She thought about the terrible scenes of Vietnam on television — bombs, shootings, victims' faces distorted in pain — and she realized that she not only had an opinion but that she was ready to express it.

"War is wrong," she said, breaking the silence. She looked

from her father to Mark, making eye contact with both. "Whether it's Vietnam or any other war, it ends up with lots of people being killed. There has to be a better way." She looked at Mark. "I don't want to see you dead," she said. Then she turned toward her older brother. "You are no coward, Matthew." Her voice cracked but she steeled herself and turned to look straight into her father's eyes before she continued. "Matthew is a pacifist. A *pacifist*, like Gandhi."

She turned back to Matthew and the two locked eyes. "That's right, Mary Clare. That's what I am." His eyes brimmed with tears but he managed a warm smile. "Thanks."

Mark didn't say a word. Dad only nodded slightly, his forehead still furrowed in deep thought. As Mary Clare carried the last of the dishes into the kitchen she was shaking a little. She had never taken a stand against her father, especially not a political stand. And though she knew her actions had nothing to do with being a saint, she couldn't help wondering if Saint Joan of Arc felt both proud and shaky when she stood up to the soldiers.

Mary Clare O'Brian
188 Jackson Street
Littleburg, Wisconsin 53538

Sister Monica, Mother Superior
Saint Mary Magdalene Convent
1123 Good Shepherd Road
Minneapolis, Minnesota 55199

May 30, 1967

Dear Reverend Mother,

It's okay that I haven't heard from you about my last letter. I know that you're really busy. But I keep having more and more questions that you're the right person to ask, because you're the most high-up-in-the-Church person I know.

One thing I wondered about was what do you think of pacifists? My oldest brother will be a conscientious objector if he gets drafted. He doesn't believe in killing and he doesn't believe the United States has any business in Vietnam. I know that we Catholics had Holy Wars to wipe out heretics. But it's a mystery to me how Catholics could justify killing people for God. I would think God would want everyone to have life. And I just can't see how we can call any war that involves killing a "Holy War."

But back to Vietnam. I was wondering how you felt because I saw some nuns on the news holding signs and protesting the war. I didn't know nuns could protest until that very moment and I was surprised. But Matthew says that in the seminary he and some of the other guys, even some priests, go on protests against the war. They march for civil rights, too. How about that?

I just wondered what you believe and whether your Good Shepherd nuns are politically involved.

Sincerely,
Mary Clare O'Brian

P.S. Only fifteen weeks until I'll be a seventh grader!
P.P.S. What do you think of torturing yourself for God — you know — Mortification of the Flesh, like the coarse shirts some saints wore, or rough itchy belts, or self-flagellation? I have to tell you, I tried a few things and I just can't do it. I tried wearing a jack (from the Jax game) in my shoe and I couldn't stand it. I also tried saying the rosary while kneeling on an old screen. It hurt too much. I sure hope you don't do this kind of thing at Good Shepherd. I asked Sister Charlotte and she said Franciscan nuns don't. Why would God want us to hurt ourselves?

Saint Mary Magdalene Convent and School
1123 Good Shepherd Road
Minneapolis, Minnesota 55199

Mary Clare O'Brian
189 Jackson St.
Littleburg, Wisconsin 53538

May, 1967

Dear Mary Clare,

If you recall, your last letters consisted of several topics: sin, the new habits your nuns are wearing, your fear that your mother is losing her faith because of Betty Freidan's book, as well as questions about why the Virgin Mary cries so often. You certainly keep me on my toes!

I'm glad you are not so focused on sin now. When the Church was primarily focused on sin, purgatory, and hell, it was because of the belief that people obey out of fear. So if people feared God they would obey. We now know that people also obey out of love and that love is a much better motivator.

I would love to see a picture of Sister Charlotte in her new habit. Many of my Sisters have asked me about new habits but I have made no decision about it yet. I plan to attend a three-day seminar that the Good Shepherd nuns will hold in Milwaukee in August where it will be discussed.

Now to your mother's loss of faith. I don't think you can blame Betty Freidan for your mother's feelings. I've read The Feminine Mystique, and though Freidan is too radical for me I think she hit a nerve with women everywhere. Even my Sisters are talking about gender roles in the Church.

Your mother has been Catholic her whole life, Mary Clare. I'm sure she'll return to her faith when she reconciles her pregnancy. Remember to pray for her daily and I'll do the same.

About the Virgin Mary always crying—I have seen numerous pictures in which Mary was not crying. When she's portrayed crying it is because she wants peace in our world and she wants people to follow God's laws. What do you feel when you see Mary crying?

Finally, your question about St. Theresa. I assume you're talking about the part in The Interior Castle *when one of the nuns kept walking over her clean floors, forcing St. Theresa to rewash them. If she had confronted the nun, they would have shared angry words. She chose to offer her additional work up to God. This seems to bother you. Can you tell me why?*

I don't have the specifics right here for my trip to Wisconsin, but I would enjoy meeting you when I come if you could get someone to take you to Milwaukee. I'll send you the dates and location soon.

Fondly,
Mother Monica

P.S. I just received your letter in which you ask about civil rights, the Vietnam war, and pacifists. I believe that all people should be respected and enjoy the same rights as everyone else. I also believe in peace. Every day I pray to God for peace and justice in the world. I also pray that the world leaders make humanitarian decisions.

11

When Carl, Dennis, and Butch arrived, Matthew whisked them off to the Pad where the band could have its privacy. The detached garage was built on a slope and the large room underneath had held nothing but junk until Matthew, Mark, and Luke cleaned it out a few years earlier. They shared it pretty well with each other, but it was understood that when Matthew was home, he got first dibs.

Mary Clare was not invited. She was never invited. In fact, Mark and Luke had told her that they would make her life miserable if they ever learned that she or her friends had been inside. So the only time she'd ventured in the Pad was when she'd had one of her friends serve as a lookout. The boys had brought in a stuffed chair and couch they'd covered with a tie-dyed sheet. They had a table with a lamp and everything. Mary Clare thought it was psychedelic.

While Mary Clare did the dishes she prayed the band would still practice in the garage so she could see them. They were such cute guys, it was almost a shame they were seminarians. But Matthew said he might not stay in the seminary, so maybe the others wouldn't, either.

What was she thinking? It was probably a big sin to have a

crush on a boy whom God had called to be a priest. Besides, if she wanted to become a saint she couldn't have a crush on *any* boy.

Mary Clare lamented that she and Joannie hadn't thought about what to do if the guys were hanging out in the Pad. Then it occurred to her: she would make brownies. Maybe that would get the guys back in the house, or, even better, get her into the Pad.

When the brownies were done Mary Clare placed them on two separate plates, one for the kids who were watching TV and one for the guys in the Pad. She brought the warm brownies to the family room first. Then she went down the slope of her backyard to the door of the Pad. Armed with her brownies, she did what she'd never dared to do before: she knocked on the door.

"Who's there?" Matthew yelled.

"I have something for you. Something you'll like."

It was Butch who opened the door, smiling what seemed a nervous smile.

"Hi, Mary Clare," he said. Behind him Carl was trying to hide some big tubular thing that had smoke coming out of it. Whatever it was, she wasn't supposed to see it.

"Hi." A waft of sweet-smelling smoke assaulted her. Her eyes began to adjust to the dimly lit room, and a girl Mary Clare had never seen before spoke up.

"Brownies! I'm starving." She had long blonde hair—straight, perfect hair, and dangly earrings. "What kind of brownies *are* those, kid?" Before Mary Clare could answer that they were the kind with walnuts, everybody—even Matthew—cracked up laughing. Mary Clare stood there feeling stupid as every last brownie disappeared. Whatever the joke was, she felt that they were making fun of her. It was clear that she didn't belong. Taking the empty plate she turned around and walked out.

"Hey," Matthew called after her when she was halfway up the hill. "There's nothing to be mad about." He was all smiles.

She knew what he was doing. He didn't want her to go back mad and tattle that the room was smoky. Or maybe, just maybe, he was being nice because she was kind to him earlier. It didn't matter. She was going to use the moment to her advantage.

"I need to talk to you," Mary Clare said.

"Okay, shoot."

A cold blast of wind made Mary Clare shiver. Neither of them were wearing coats.

"Just a second." Matthew ran back to the Pad and yelled for a blanket. A second later he caught the one someone threw to him and wrapped it around her shoulders.

"What's that smell?" she asked, sniffing the sweetness.

"It's an herb," he said. "Like basil or oregano or ..."

"Or marijuana," Mary Clare said. She had just figured it out.

"Geesh!" Matthew opened his mouth in shock. "Where'd you learn about marijuana—in Catholic school?"

"No, on the news. Where'd you learn about it—in the seminary?"

Matthew laughed. "Don't get any ideas, little sister. It's not for you."

Mary Clare completely forgot the words that she and Joannie had rehearsed.

"What?" he asked as she hesitated. He laughed again, an easy, relaxed laugh, so different from the tension and anger she'd seen from him at the dinner table. Mary Clare decided that she'd never find him in a better mood and decided to dive in.

"I want to have a party—just a few girlfriends. And I want The Seminarians to play."

"Ugh," was all he said. He scrunched his face like he'd smelled something bad.

"Never mind," Mary Clare said. "If Dad yelled like he did tonight, he'd just embarrass me anyway." She felt tired suddenly, deflated. "It was just a dumb idea." She looked across the lawn at the patch of ground that would soon become the vegetable garden.

Matthew didn't say anything for a minute. He stood looking up at the stars. Mary Clare was about to turn around and walk into the house when he surprised her.

"You know, I think I could get the guys to do this. I think they'll be fine with it. And you don't have to worry about Dad. He's not going to yell if there's a party. He likes listening to the band."

"But what about Mom? What about the baby?"

Matthew let out his breath in a long stream, slowly shaking his head back and forth. "Yeah, I know. It makes me sick. Another baby could kill her. But the way she took on the old man tonight, I think she'll be okay."

Mary Clare stopped breathing, stopped thinking. It was like someone had shoved icicles in her veins. "Kill her?"

Matthew shrugged. "I don't know. How much do you think that body of hers can take?" Matthew noticed her panic-stricken face and placed his hand on Mary Clare's shoulder. "No. I didn't mean that she'd literally die, it's just—she doesn't want another baby, that's all."

Neither said anything for a long time. It was Mary Clare who finally broke the silence. "She has to be okay. She has to be." Mary Clare envisioned trying to take care of the kids by herself when Dad was gone. Matthew would be off at the seminary. Mark and Luke would do whatever they wanted to and everything would fall on her shoulders. She sat on the cold, wet ground.

Matthew squatted down next to her. "You know what I think would make Mom feel better?"

Mary Clare shook her head.

"A party. You know how she loves to entertain. It would give her something else to think about. Maybe she'd even make some fancy appetizers," Matthew said with a grin.

Mary Clare thought of all the cocktail and dinner parties her parents had given over the years and how much fun it was to help them get ready.

"Maybe we should wait till she's over her morning sickness," Mary Clare said.

Matthew nodded. "Yup, maybe in July or August."

Mary Clare stood up and hugged her big brother. He laughed.

"I have something to tell you too. I applied for CO status today."

"CO?" repeated Mary Clare, puzzled.

"Conscientious Objector," Matthew explained. "If I get approved I won't have to worry about fighting a war. One of the priests at the seminary said he'd write a letter explaining my beliefs. That should help. So anyway, pray that I get approved."

"Okay," Mary Clare said. But she wasn't really thinking about praying, she was wondering something else. "Are you going back to the seminary now that you're graduating?"

He chuckled. "No way. But don't go talking about me applying for CO or not going back to the seminary to Mom and Dad or anybody, okay?"

"Okay," Mary Clare said. But she couldn't wait to tell Joannie and start a list of song requests.

12

Mary Clare was still shaking as she collapsed on her bed. She listened for the sound of the phone ringing or the doorbell chiming. Either one could mean that Mrs. Turner was contacting her parents and she'd be in trouble.

Trouble? She'd been trying to do a good thing, a holy thing.

From somewhere downstairs she could hear her mother singing a silly song about an ant trying to move a rubber-tree plant. "But he had high hopes, he had hi-igh-igh hopes, he had high apple-pie-in-the-sky-y-y hopes. So every time you're feeling bad, 'stead of feeling sad, just remember that ant. Oops, there goes another rubber tree! Oops, there goes another rubber tree! Oops, there goes another rubber-tree plant! Ker-plant!" Her voice rang out strong and cheerful, the way it used to before all the anger and sadness of the last months. Maybe God was finally noticing Mary Clare's good works and making her mom better.

Not that Mrs. Turner would see her as a good person.

"I don't want to see your face in this yard or near my daughter again. Do you hear me?"

Mary Clare did hear her and she said so. Then she ran up the hill as fast as her legs could carry her, tripping just once on the jagged sidewalk in front of the Brown's and hitting her right knee hard on the sidewalk. Now it was bruised and bleeding.

But what had she done that was so terrible anyway? She'd been talking with Becky Turner and Tina Anderson about being Catholic. To bring them into the fold would be a saintly thing to do, and Mary Clare certainly needed saint points.

It had all started in Becky's parents' pop-up trailer that was set up in the backyard. They had permission to play in there as long as they didn't bring in anything to eat or drink.

But when Tina brought Jiffy Pop she and Mary Clare had made before they came over, Becky said it was okay. "My mom is at a meeting this afternoon, and she never comes back here anyway." They made a pitcher of grape Kool-Aid and filled tall tumblers to enjoy with the popcorn.

The three listened to WLS from Chicago, playing "The Best of the 60s So Far" on Tina's transistor radio, and they sang along with the familiar songs from Bob Dylan, The Monkees, and The Singing Nun. The girls had all seen her on the Ed Sullivan show singing "Dominique, nique, nique . . ." which was the only part they could sing along with her because it was in French.

Hearing it now had to be a sign from God. Mary Clare was supposed to bring up Catholicism.

She didn't have to.

"That song is so cool," Becky said.

"I think nuns are cool. I love their habits. I just wish you didn't have to be a Catholic to become a nun," Tina said. She brought a buttery handful of popcorn to her mouth, dropping half of it on the floor.

"What's wrong with Catholics?" Mary Clare asked. "You know it *is* the true religion."

"What does that mean?" Tina asked.

"It means you have to be Catholic . . ."

130

Becky interrupted. "I heard some bad things about nuns and priests."

Mary Clare was shocked. "Bad things about nuns and priests?" She tried to think what the bad things could be. "You mean how strict they can be?"

"No, not *that* kind of bad. Worse," Becky said. "I heard that priests and nuns sleep in the same bed together, and that ..."

"That's ridiculous!" Mary Clare blurted. "Priests and nuns can't even get married."

Just then Mrs. Turner's face appeared in the screen door. She let herself in and stood with hands on hips. Mary Clare looked at Becky. Her face went pale and she kept her eyes on the floor, where several ants had already discovered the spilled popcorn. Mary Clare was sure Becky was in big trouble until she heard her own name in Mrs. Turner's angry voice.

"Mary Clare O'Brian! Are you trying to convert my daughter to Catholicism?" Mrs. Turner's chubby cheeks were fire-truck red. She had never appeared so formidable. "Well?" she demanded.

Mary Clare couldn't say no. This was a moment of truth. It was the kind of question the saints and martyrs died for. This was her chance to be a soldier for Christ and to stand up for her faith. She thought of St. Peter, who had denied Christ three times before the cock crowed. She thought of how ashamed he had been. She had to speak the truth.

"Yes, ma'am, I am." Her voice was a bit squeaky, but it got stronger. "I want them to be able to go to heaven and they have to be Catholic in order to do that."

Mrs. Turner laughed an ugly, angry laugh. "Everybody thinks their religion is the true religion. Don't you know that?"

No, Mary Clare did not know that. Actually she'd given very little thought to how other religions thought of themselves.

"If you think these wonderful girls won't be welcome in the Kingdom of Heaven—well, girly-girl, you've just been brainwashed. If the truth be known, the Catholics are the bad lot."

Mary Clare was trying to back up toward the door of the trailer when she heard those horrible words.

"That's right," Mrs. Turner said. "You go home now and don't come back here with your religious plots."

Mary Clare listened for the phone or doorbell as she cleaned up her knee with soap and water. It hurt, but not anywhere near as much as her heart hurt. Had she done the right thing trying to convert Becky and Tina? If she'd done what God wanted her to do, why did it hurt so much? She'd always imagined the saints and martyrs feeling pious when they stood up for God. When she used to play martyr, as a child, she would stand tall against her persecutors (usually Mark and Luke) with righteous indignation, strength, and determination. She would turn to the crowd and offer wisdom before they beheaded her. But in her imagination, the persecutors were Roman soldiers and other non-believers. They weren't real people. Now, in real life, the Turners were not only real people, they lived down the street. She did not feel righteous indignation. More like humiliation.

And what about Tina and Becky? They hadn't said one word in her defense. They could have said, "Mary Clare is cool. We like hearing what she has to say." Not a peep. Tina Anderson had stared at her limp, lap-hugging hands when Mrs. Turner was lecturing, and Becky had scrambled to pick up popcorn, never looking at Mary Clare or her mother.

Unless this was a test. It could be that she was meant to stand up for her religion and did do the right thing. Mary Clare lay down on her bed, hearing Mrs. Turner's words over and over in her head: "Everyone thinks their religion is the true religion." If that was true, then maybe Catholics were—no, she didn't want to think about that possibility. She would have to take this to a higher authority.

Mary Clare O'Brian
188 Jackson Street
Littleburg, Wisconsin 53538

Sister Monica, Mother Superior
Saint Mary Magdalene Convent
1123 Good Shepherd Road
Minneapolis, Minnesota 55199

May 24, 1967

Dear Reverend Mother,

I was trying to convert the neighbors who are non-Catholic but it turned out badly. They think horrible things about the Catholic Church that I never knew anybody thought. And they don't even believe that it's the true faith. Should I keep trying to convert them?

Sometimes the way God works doesn't make any sense at all. I know I shouldn't say things like that but it's true. Just when we were all accepting God's will, He goes and changes His mind. Nobody was happy that Mom was going to have another baby, but that didn't mean we wanted her to lose it. So why would God let her get pregnant and then take away the baby? Mom is all pasty white and doesn't show any feelings at all.

You don't think she lost the baby because nobody was happy about it, do you?

Sincerely,
Mary Clare

13

It was the last day of school. Mary Clare looked around the classroom at twenty kids in shorts and tee shirts—at school! The rest of the kids, including Mary Clare, still had to change. They had worn their uniform to morning Mass, of course, but were told to wear shorts under their skirts or pants and to bring along a suitable blouse or tee shirt for the school picnic.

It was mighty cool out for the last day of school and the clouds threatened rain, but that didn't mean the picnic would be cancelled. The nuns seemed to look forward to these outings more than the kids—especially kids like Mary Clare, who dreaded the sports activities. Still, Mary Clare thought, it was the official end of school and it would be great to get outdoors. She tried to make herself get excited about it, but she'd been dragging all morning.

"Row four, you may go," Sister Charlotte said.

Row four started for the door. Mary Clare's row would be called next.

"Whatcha doing this summer?" Gregory asked.

"Not too much. We go to Rock Lake three or four days a week."

"Gee, you're lucky. I hardly ever get to the beach. Well …"

Gregory developed a sudden interest in his shoelaces. "Maybe we'll run into each other somewhere."

"We will, because I'm going to have a party," Mary Clare said, realizing at that very moment that she would also invite boys. From the corner of her eye she could see that Jen and Sandy and Kelly were all listening. "With a live band."

"You're kidding," Jen said.

"Wow," Sandy said.

"You didn't tell me," Kelly said.

Mary Clare held her chin just a little higher than usual. She knew that everybody would want to come to a party with a live band. It seemed so grown-up. She still hadn't gotten permission—but all in good time. Though she had always been on the edge of popularity and was invited to most things, it had been harder since everybody knew her family had money problems—and especially since befriending the bag-lunchers. Even Kelly seemed less and less interested in being her friend. She did have Joannie, and Joannie was becoming a great friend. But she wanted everyone to like her. This party would really help.

"Row five," Sister Charlotte said.

When Mary Clare stepped out of the classroom to take her turn in the bathroom, a sharp pain pierced her side. She hoped no one saw her place her hand over the painful area protectively. By the time she got into a stall in the bathroom her stomach was cramping violently. She thought she might throw up.

I must have the flu, she thought. But when she saw the stain on her panties, she knew that it wasn't the flu. She thought back to the special presentation Sister Charlotte had given earlier in the year. It was a special mother/daughter meeting and all the girls received a booklet, *Growing Up and Liking It*.

Mary Clare had hidden it first under her coat and then in

the closet under her box of glow-in-the-dark statues. She hadn't thought about it much since.

The cramping subsided as quickly as it had started, but Mary Clare knew that there was no way she was going to the picnic. She wasn't going to wear her tan shorts home either. Not without keeping her dark skirt on over them.

When she felt strong enough, Mary Clare returned to the classroom. But just long enough to stand in the doorway and motion Sister Charlotte into the hallway.

"I ... I'm ... I have to go home," she said.

Sister Charlotte's brow furrowed. "Are you sick?"

Mary Clare nodded. She could feel her face heat up, which seemed to tell Sister Charlotte everything.

"Is this your first time?"

Mary Clare nodded. She wanted to sink through the floor.

Sister smiled warmly, her dimples showing. "I have something for you then," she said. "Wait in the girls' bathroom."

Mary Clare couldn't imagine what Sister Charlotte had to smile about. But she proceeded to the girls' bathroom and was grateful to find it empty. Row five had finished changing and Sister hadn't called row six yet.

Sister returned with a small white bag. Inside were the supplies they had learned about months before.

"Do you feel up to going to the picnic?"

"No," Mary Clare said in a small voice. She would simply die if anyone knew.

"Then do you feel well enough to walk home by yourself?"

Mary Clare nodded. It wasn't a very confident nod, but she didn't have much of a choice. Dad was out of town with the car.

Mary Clare was surprised that she felt fine on the walk home. Her cramps were gone almost as soon as they'd started. She considered the pros and cons of how her day had changed so quickly. She didn't have to go to the class picnic and participate in silly games or races. She got almost a whole day off, and since Johnny and Mom were the only ones home it would be a quiet day. But on the other hand, she wasn't sure she liked what was happening in her body. She wondered what her classmates thought of her sudden disappearance. And home wasn't the best place to be when the whole family—even Mom—even the house itself—was drenched in the doom and gloom of a lost baby.

It wasn't as if anybody really talked about it much. Gabby, of course, had to ask if it would have been a boy or a girl, which made Mom burst into tears all over again. "It was too soon to know," she'd told Gabby. Dad's eyes were far away most of the time he was home. He only mentioned it on the night she lost the baby, when he led the whole family in the rosary. He had been really sweet to their mother though, hugging her and sitting with her. Mom herself had been impossible to figure out. One minute she'd be in tears, the next minute she'd yell at someone, and all of a sudden she'd be laughing.

Mary Clare could hear the *click click* of Mom's typewriter when she entered the front door. She followed the sound to the dining room, where her mother paused to take a drag off her cigarette before returning to her typing. Little Johnny saw her first. He knocked over a pile of Tinker Toys hurrying to greet her. Mary Clare lifted him into her arms and kissed his cheeks.

"What are you doing home?" her mother asked. She quickly reached for the plastic typewriter cover and slipped it on, covering the machine and the sheet of paper she'd been typing. "Tell me," she added.

Mary Clare wondered what her mother was covering up. She started to consider what to say, but to her own surprise she burst into tears instead.

"Oh, honey!" Mom reached out her arms and Mary Clare went to them.

When she had gathered herself together enough to tell her mother what was going on, she discovered that her mother was smiling back at her.

"This is great!" her mother said. "It means that you're a woman. It means that someday when you're married, you'll be able to have babies."

Mary Clare felt ... she didn't know what she felt. So many feelings to sort out and they were all wound up like the inside of a tennis ball. It would take a long time to unravel them all.

"Mary Clare, it's a great thing to be able to have babies," her mother said.

"But the baby you lost ..."

Her mother shook her head. "It was too much for me, too much for this family. I think God knew that. It just wasn't meant to be. But you do know that I wanted you." She squinted her eyes. "I wanted all of you."

Mary Clare nodded. Of course she knew that.

"But what if I want to become a nun?" Mary Clare thought about her *Growing Up and Liking It* pamphlet. She thought about all the eggs that women carried in their ovaries.

"Then you won't have babies."

Mary Clare considered this. "But I don't know if I could waste all those eggs."

Her mother laughed. At the same time Johnny squealed as if he were in on the joke. Though she hadn't meant to be funny, Mary Clare loved the sound of her mother's laughter. Her mother picked up Johnny and headed toward the kitchen.

"Come on in here, Mary Clare. I'm going to make us some lunch. And why don't you open up some windows? We could use some fresh air in here."

Part 2
Summer

14

When summer vacation started Mary Clare could think of nothing she wanted to do more than spend a day at Rock Lake. Even if the temperature was only 74 degrees. Even if the water was still too cold to swim in. Even if her older brothers were all busy and she'd end up watching the little kids most of the day. As far as Mary Clare was concerned, when her family made their first trek to the beach with a picnic lunch and swimsuits it really and truly felt like summer.

Mary Clare loved the easy attitude everybody seemed to have at the beach. Especially her parents. All the tension and worry seemed to melt away out in the open air. Her father might even join them since he was working out of his home office today.

"Can we please go?" Mary Clare begged.

"I guess so," Mom said when Mary Clare made her case. "We may not be able to go very often this summer."

Mary Clare was already halfway out of the room to get ready, but she stopped.

"Why not?"

"Never mind. I'm going to talk to your father, then I'm off to the grocery store. You organize the kids and start packing the beach stuff. I'll see if Dad can come too."

Mary Clare loved that her mother was finally in a good mood. She hoped that her actions were contributing to that mood. Since summer began, Mary Clare had poured her heart and soul into cleaning and baking and taking care of the little kids.

While Mom was at the grocery store shopping for picnic food and charcoal, Mary Clare corralled the kids and told them about the beach. Anne and Gabby agreed to dress the little kids while Mary Clare gathered all the beach things that hadn't been used since last summer.

By the time Mom got home with the food, Mary Clare had organized the beach towels, swimsuits, and sweaters for everyone in case it got colder, and she had rinsed out the big metal ice chest Dad retrieved from the garage. She even remembered the director's chairs Mom and Dad liked to sit in at the lake.

By 11:00 the family was ready to go. The kids piled into the car, so grateful for the trip that no one complained about where they were sitting or how squished they were.

"Roll call," Dad announced as he backed out of the driveway. Roll call was a trip ritual they had started when Margaret was accidentally left behind at the Gallagher farm the year before last.

"Matthew," Dad called, even though he knew Matthew was working. The ritual required that he name each of the kids in order of age.

"Absent," the kids all yelled.

"Mark," Dad called.

"Absent," the kids yelled.

"Luke," Dad called.

"Absent," the kids yelled again. By the time Mary Clare, Anne, Gabby, Margaret, Martha, and Johnny piped in with "Here!" in response to their names, Dad was on the highway.

"Let's say a prayer for a safe trip," Dad said. He began the

Memorare. Everyone except Johnny recited the prayer from memory.

Dad always led the prayer and today was no exception. "Remember, oh most Gracious Virgin Mary, that never was it known, that anyone who fled to thy protection, implored thy help, or sought thy intercession was left unaided. Inspired by this confidence, I fly unto thee, oh Virgin of virgins my Mother. To thee I come, before thee I stand, sinful and sorrowful. Oh Mother of the Word Incarnate, despise not my petition, but in thy mercy hear and answer me. Amen."

Margaret was sitting on Mary Clare's lap, making it easy for Mary Clare to hear her sister's mistakes. "Margaret," Mary Clare said, "it's not 'Almost gracious Virgin Mary,' it's 'Oh most gracious Virgin Mary.'"

"Ohhhhhh," Margaret said. The other kids giggled.

"And it's not 'that never wasn't known,'" Mary Clare said. "The words are 'that never was it known that anyone who fled to thy protection ...'"

Margaret pouted. "It still doesn't make any sense," she said. "It's a dumb prayer."

Mary Clare was so shocked that she jerked straight up in her seat, making Margaret tumble from her lap into Gabby, who was sitting on the floor beneath them.

"Ow!" Gabby said.

Margaret started crying.

"What's going on back there?" both parents yelled.

"I didn't mean to drop her," Mary Clare protested. "But did you hear her? She committed a sacrilege! She called the Memorare dumb, and that's a sin."

Now Margaret started crying harder.

"It's okay, Margaret," Mom said softly.

Dad took it from there. "The Memorare is an old traditional

prayer that you grow into as you get older. I didn't understand it when I was a boy—in fact, I thought it was a foreign language." He gave Mary Clare a hard, warning look in the rearview mirror. "All you need to know right now, Margaret, is that we're asking the Virgin Mary to protect us."

Mary Clare nodded. She held Margaret as gently as she could and looked out the window at the green, rolling hills, the cornfields with newly formed stalks, the red barns and fenced-in areas holding all sorts of farm animals—cows and sheep, horses, chickens, pigs. Everyone was quiet as they drove the last ten minutes of the twenty-minute drive. But the minute they pulled into Rock Park and could see the lake, everyone came alive again.

There were only a dozen or so people at the lake, and Mary Clare could only make out three who were swimming. The reason was immediately apparent. The breeze that had been gentle in Littleburg was downright chilly coming off the lake.

"Find a nice place to set up in the sun," Dad said. "And forget about putting on your suits. There'll be no swimming today."

Mary Clare wanted to cry. This was not at all what she had pictured. She had put on her two-piece swimsuit under her clothes, so she could rip her clothes off and jump into the water first thing. Swimming was her favorite thing in the world. She loved opening her eyes under water and exploring all the mysteries it held. This year she was determined to swim all the way out to the raft where the teenagers played. It would make her feel cool, like she was one of them. The little kids loved the water too. Now they'd probably be whiney and difficult all day.

As soon as everything was unloaded Dad excused himself to go to the men's room, which was way on the other side of the grounds. Mary Clare started toward the water with all the kids in tow behind her.

"Wait, Mary Clare," Mom said. "You stay here. I want to talk to you." She cupped her hands over her mouth to be heard. "Anne, you're in charge of the little kids!" Anne turned and nodded.

Mary Clare looked out at the water wistfully. She rubbed her arms against the goose bumps that rose from the cold air.

"Sit down," Mom said, motioning to the two director's chairs. "I've got to talk to you before your father gets back."

Mom leaned forward, her eyes intent on Mary Clare. "I've made a big decision. And before I talk to your father about it, I wanted to tell you because — well, because how you feel about this will make a big difference in whether or not your father will accept it."

Mary Clare couldn't imagine how her opinion could be so important. She turned to see where her father was. He was walking casually toward the bathroom and was only about halfway across the park. They had a little bit of time. "What?" she asked. She couldn't imagine where this was leading.

"You know that I've been really depressed lately."

Mary Clare nodded. "Yeah, but you seem better today."

"I *am* better today." She reached over and took both of Mary Clare's hands in her own. "The reason I'm better is because I figured out how I can solve some of our money problems."

Mary Clare made a little gasp of surprise. Her prayers, her sacrifices, they were working!

"I got a job! Oh, Mary Clare, it's going to make such a difference for our family. It's not just any job either, it's a teaching position!"

"Oh," Mary Clare said. That was all she could think of to say.

She tried to imagine her mother with a job, but she couldn't. Nobody's mother had jobs. She remembered last week when her mother had raged at the television during a commercial for toilet bowl cleaner. The prissy lady in the commercial was wearing a dress and high heels and a pearl necklace as she cleaned the toilet. "Don't you think for one minute," Mom had yelled, "that that lady is smiling because she's cleaning out a toilet bowl. She's smiling because she's making a commercial and getting paid good money for it." Mary Clare and her sisters had looked at each other in amazement. Gabby had made the crazy sign with her finger circling her ear. Mary Clare had wondered, for the first time, if her mother resented not making money.

Mom pulled a cigarette out of her pocket and lit it. The smoke curled in little rings as she exhaled. "I asked Father Dwyer if there would be a teaching position at Maria Goretti School, and he said he'd just learned they would need a lay teacher."

"*My school?* You can't — wait, which teacher's leaving?"

"I honestly don't know. Father Dwyer wasn't at liberty to tell me. I only know that I'd be teaching one of the upper grades. Mary Clare, with the salary I'd be making we would have enough money for the first time in years. At first Father had reservations about me because I don't have a degree and because he'd heard I was expecting. But since I lost the baby ..."

Mary Clare nodded, staring at her feet.

"I know it's going to be difficult with me gone all day. I'm going to have to depend on you to help even more around the house — starting dinner and that kind of thing."

"But Dad's gonna ..."

"You're right," Mom blurted. "Your father is going to have a tough time with this. I'm going to have to prove to him that the family will be better off with me working and showing him that you're behind me. Mary Clare, if you have a good attitude about me working and show your father that you're confident every-thing will be okay at home, I'll have an easier time convincing him about the job."

"Help out more?" Mary Clare couldn't imagine what more she could be expected to do. She couldn't imagine her mother teaching at her school. She looked out over the water and at her sisters playing in the sand at the shore, and for a moment she stopped trying to think at all.

"Your father's coming. And there's more I have to tell you."

Mary Clare looked into her mother's eyes. They sparkled in a way she hadn't seen for a long time.

"I have to go to summer school too."

"What?" Mary Clare gripped the arms of the director's chair. This was ridiculous. Who ever heard of a forty-year-old woman going to school! She glanced in the direction of her father and saw that he was halfway back from the bathroom.

"Yes, even parochial school teachers will have to have a degree in three years. So I promised Father Dwyer that I could squeeze a year of college into three summers."

"What about the boys?" Even as she said it, Mary Clare knew this was a ridiculous option. They were guys. They had never been expected to do much around the house, and they would balk at housework.

"They all have jobs this summer, Mary Clare. They have to save for college." She laughed. "And can you imagine what the house would be like ..."

Mary Clare locked her hands over her forehead and closed her eyes. She couldn't begin to sort out all the pieces—Mom back in school, Mom teaching at her school, even more responsibility.

Leaning forward again, Mom and Mary Clare locked eyes. "Please, Mary Clare, help me help our family."

"Sure," Mary Clare heard herself say. It wasn't that she had thought her mother's request through. She would have said "sure" to anything Mom asked right then. "Sure" meant her mother's eyes would continue to sparkle. "Sure" meant she would continue to hear excitement in her mother's voice, and laughter and enthusiasm too. "Sure" meant the promise—or at least the hope of the promise—that her mother would be a happy person. And if Mom was happy, the whole family would be okay.

Saint Mary Magdalene Convent and School
1123 Good Shepherd Road
Minneapolis, Minnesota 55199

Mary Clare O'Brian
188 Jackson St.
Littleburg, Wisconsin 53538

June, 1967

Dear Mary Clare,

I was so very sad to hear about your mother in your last letters. First
you wrote about her crisis of faith. Then you wrote about her losing
the baby and the difficult emotions, I imagine, that your whole family
faced. I'm sorry that things have been so hard.

People struggle their whole lives trying to understand God's will.
Some people think that God plans every little thing that happens to
us. Those people think that if someone snubs us, or offers us a piece
of cake, it happened because God willed it to happen. I don't see it
that way. I think that many things happen because God gave us free
will, and with all that freedom, we created an imperfect world where
things happen sometimes because of mean-spiritedness, sometimes
because of kindness, and sometimes by accident.

I don't know what went wrong with the baby that made your
mother lose it, but I have many unwed mothers at our Good
Shepherd home that never wanted to have a baby — and if wishing
the baby away had worked, they wouldn't be here.

As for your mother losing her faith, I am praying for her but I'm
not terribly worried. Mary Clare, part of free will is that we *choose*
God. To really choose God we have to question our own beliefs from
time to time. And sometimes life crises lead to a crisis in faith. Your

mother has followed Catholic teachings her whole life. When she finds God again, she may change some of the particulars of her faith, but her faith will be deeper. That's just the way it works.

I think that your Spiritual Bouquet for your mother is wonderful, but don't forget to hold simple conversations with God as well.

My love and prayers,
Mother Monica

P.S. About converting your neighbors—for heaven sakes! You're going to start a Holy War. Remember that Pope John XXIII wanted us to be more accepting of others.

15

Mary Clare wiped down the kitchen counter, enjoying the delicious knowledge that the rest of the day was hers to enjoy any way she wanted. It was Sunday. Mom had been in school for two long weeks and was now sitting at the kitchen table writing out a schedule of meals for the upcoming week. Dad was attending a conference in Michigan and Mark and Luke were camping at Devil's Lake with some friends. The kids were all playing outside.

The first few days after Mom told Dad about her plan to go back to school and teach had been tumultuous to say the least. Mary Clare listened as Dad used every argument he could think of to dissuade her mother from her plan.

"Our kids will be orphans," he said at one point. Mom reminded him that they still had two parents. "People will be saying terrible things about you," he told her. She said she was ready to handle it. "What makes you think that after all these years you can step back into the university and make decent grades?" Mom said she'd die if she didn't try. "We can't afford for you to go back to school." Mom had an answer for that, too. She had gotten a scholarship.

"My scholarship not only pays for tuition but includes a living stipend. We'll be better off financially before I even start working," Mom said.

That silenced Dad but it didn't make him happy. Dad couldn't argue about how much she'd be earning with her job either. Mary Clare saw the charts and tables her Mom had generated, showing how they would pay off each bill with the income she'd start earning in the fall. She listened from the kitchen as her mom appealed to Dad's Achilles' heel.

"I don't want you to have the burden of all the finances anymore. All these children, and you providing for them without help," she said.

When the phone rang, Mary Clare wiped her hands dry on her shorts and ran to pick it up.

"Whatcha doin?" Mary Clare recognized Jen's voice.

"Nothing much, unless you count housework."

"She's doing housework," Jen said to an invisible audience.

"Yuck, tell her to break free." It was Kelly's voice.

Mary Clare felt her insides clench. Kelly had hung out with her during the first few days Mom was in school. She had even helped out. But one day she'd found it all too much. When Mary Clare would call her she was always too busy. Now Mary Clare realized that Kelly was hanging out with the rest of the group. She may have even defected as Mary Clare's best friend.

"I hear you've been doing nothing but working this summer. Is that true?" Jen asked.

"Yup." Mary Clare wanted to throw the phone at something. It was so unfair. Her friends were having a normal summer of swimming and fun while she was stuck at home. She tried to keep her voice even. "Who's all there?"

"Just Kelly and Sandy," Jen said. "My brother said he'd take us to Lake Ripley tomorrow and we wanted to see if you could come."

"Rats!" Mary Clare said. "I could do it today. I have this afternoon off."

Jen laughed. "Mary Clare has the afternoon *off*," she repeated to their friends. Mary Clare could hear laughter in the background. "Gosh, you sound like a maid or a slave or something."

Mary Clare swallowed the hard lump of anger and self-pity that was rising in her throat. She didn't appreciate being laughed at and was about to say so.

"Today won't work, Mary Clare. We've all got family stuff going on later."

"Let me tell her about the party," she could hear Sandy say. "Hey, Mary Clare, I'm having a slumber party Wednesday night. I told my mom it's all I want for my birthday."

"That sounds fun," Mary Clare said. "I'll have to talk to my mom. I just hope she doesn't have play practice that night."

"Play practice?" Sandy asked.

"Yeah, Mom's in Summer Stock Theater. She gets three credits for acting but she has to practice at night sometimes."

"Oh," Sandy said. "Well, I sure hope you can come."

"I'll call you back as soon as I know." Mary Clare braced herself for talking to Mom. She said a quick prayer begging God to make it so she could go to the party.

Mom was putting the last touches on the meal chart for the following week when Mary Clare approached her. "Do you want to come with me to the grocery store?" Mom asked. "We'll get everything you need for the week."

"No," Mary Clare blurted. "I want to do something *fun* but everybody's busy." She flung herself dramatically onto a kitchen chair.

"Hmm," her mom said. "I just thought you might want to spend a little time together. We haven't had much time lately."

That was an understatement. The play meant that Mom was

away early in the morning until late at night some days. Mary Clare let out a sigh.

"Sandy's having a slumber party on Wednesday," she said. "It's for her birth ..."

But Mom was already shaking her head. "Out of the question," she said. "I have play practice that night, and your father will still be out of town."

"It's not fair!" Mary Clare yelled. "Somebody else is going to have to stay home. Or you can hire a babysitter." Mary Clare stomped out of the room and up the stairs, ignoring her mother's pleading voice from the kitchen.

"I know it's not fair. I'm sorry. Please don't start. I need your cooperation."

But this was too much for Mary Clare. She threw herself on her bed and sobbed angry tears. *This was not the deal, God. When I said I'd be a saint, I didn't think it meant working every minute of every single day and giving up my friends. How could you expect this of me?* Mary Clare wasn't sure that it was right to talk to God this way, but she couldn't make herself stop. *I thought you would make miracles happen—maybe Dad would get a big raise, or a huge anonymous check would appear in the mail. I thought maybe somebody would pay for our house and all the bills would magically disappear. But Mom going back to school and getting a job— that's no miracle. It's Mom solving the problem instead of you. You're not doing your part, God. You're not.*

Mary Clare was pretty sure that she had gone too far talking to God that way. She had gone from being saintlike to being bad, just like that. But it still didn't stop the angry tears. Now she wondered if she'd end up in purgatory for a long, long time—or even worse. And it would be six days before she could go to confession.

It took a few minutes for Mary Clare to pull herself together so she could call Jen back. Sandy had already gone home, so she told Jen the bad news.

"We were talking about this," Jen said. "It's not fair."

"I know," Mary Clare said.

"Do you want my mom to call her?"

"Your mom?"

"Yeah. She thinks your mother is being self ... She thinks you're having to do your mom's job and it's really unfair. We all think that."

"No!" Mary Clare said. "Don't have your mom call." The idea made her cringe. Mary Clare knew that people were saying mean things about her mother. Mom had had arguments with both of her closest friends, who believed that women shouldn't work outside the home. One of them had even told her that it was God's will for the family to be poor and she needed to accept it. Mom said her friends had nearly broken her heart but she knew she was doing the right thing.

Now Mary Clare just wanted to change the subject. "So who's all going to be at the party?" she asked.

Jen laughed. "That's the fun part. Some of the guys found out, and Sandy thinks we can probably sneak them into the basement for a while."

"You're kidding!" This put the party on a whole new level. "Will Gregory be there?"

"Sure, he's the one who thought of crashing the party."

Mary Clare felt stabbed. She had never admitted, even to herself, that she liked Gregory, but now it seemed outrageous that her friends got to party with him without her.

"What about *your* party?" Jen asked.

"I don't know," Mary Clare said. "Anyway, I'll let you know if there's a miracle and I can come."

"Okay," Jen said.

Mary Clare was suddenly exhausted. She wanted to go to the party and resented her responsibility at home, but she didn't want people talking about her mother as if she were a bad person. She wanted to give the party with the Seminarian band but didn't know if she'd make it through all the hoops she'd have to get through to make it happen. She laid back down on the bed and fell asleep.

She awoke to the sound of Matthew's voice downstairs. His voice was animated and loud and Mom's was reassuring in the background, but Mary Clare couldn't make out what either was saying. She pulled herself out of bed and hurried downstairs.

"What happened to you?" Matthew asked when he looked at Mary Clare. "You look like you've been crying all day."

Mary Clare ducked into the main-floor bathroom. He was right. Her eyes were swollen and red. She splashed some cold water over her face and patted it dry.

"You can't do this," Mom was saying to Matthew. She was leaning against the kitchen counter next to the four loaves of bread that were almost done rising on the counter. The kitchen table was strewn with Mom's school books and paper. "You won't be able to come back."

"Back from where?" Mary Clare asked.

Matthew tried to say something in response but it came out as a croak. He pulled two envelopes out of his back pocket and tossed them to Mary Clare. She sat down at the table. The first was from The United States Selective Services. Inside was an official-looking paper. In bold letters it said "ORDER TO REPORT FOR ARMED FORCES PHYSICAL EXAMINATION." Underneath were Matthew's name and address and the ominous words, "You are hereby directed to present yourself for Armed Forces Physical Examination by reporting to the Jefferson County Courthouse, Jefferson, Wisconsin, on June 30, 1967, at 7:00 a.m."

"June thirty was Friday," Mary Clare said. "Did you go?"

"Yeah, I went," Matthew said. "I *had* to go." He slammed his fist on the counter. "But I'm not going to stick around to get my draft notice!" Mary Clare watched as the air went out of all four loaves of bread. She stifled a giggle. But when Matthew saw the bread he laughed too.

Mom rolled her eyes. "If you want to punch something, punch that dough. We'll have to knead it all over again."

"I don't understand, Matthew," Mary Clare said. "I thought you applied to become a conscientious objector."

"I did." He pointed to the other letter he had tossed to Mary Clare. "I was denied."

And Mary Clare didn't know what to say.

"He was denied," Mom said, punching some dough, "but he has appealed and may still be approved." She faced Matthew. "But if you go to Canada, you'll have problems for the rest of your life."

Matthew washed and dried his hands and took the lump of dough Mom handed him. He punched it several times, then turned to Mary Clare. "This is actually a good release," he admitted.

He kept punching the dough. "I couldn't kill anybody," he said. "I couldn't live with myself if I did." He placed the dough back into the loaf pan and dumped out another. "Father Weisman wrote a great letter for me. I sent it along with my appeal."

"That's wonderful," Mom said.

"Yeah," Matthew said. His eyes held hope. "From what I hear, I probably have a month before I get my induction notice. I guess I can wait a few weeks before I go to Canada."

"Thank you," Mom said. She kissed his forehead.

"Besides," Matthew said, looking at Mary Clare affectionately, "I owe Mary Clare a party."

"What?" Mom asked.

"We've been talking about it since before you lost the baby," Matthew said. "Mary Clare wants a party, and I said we'd play for her."

Mom grabbed her calendar. "What a wonderful idea," she said. "If we could give the party in late August I'll be home and can make pizza."

Mary Clare glowed. Everybody loved her mom's pizza.

"You look a little better than you did when I first got here," Matthew said. "So what was your problem anyway?"

"It was ..." Mary Clare couldn't bring herself to finish the sentence. She thought about the terrible decisions Matthew was facing: going to war to kill or be killed, escaping to Canada or continuing to struggle for his CO status. The fact that she was missing out on a friend's birthday party was minor in comparison.

"Something silly," she finally said.

"Okay," he said. He reached over and pinched her cheek. "So how many kids can I expect at this party?" he asked.

Mary Clare's enthusiasm returned. She'd have the best party anyone from Maria Goretti School had ever had. "Lots," she said. "I'm going to invite the whole class—girls and boys!"

Saint Mary Magdalene Convent and School
1123 Good Shepherd Road
Minneapolis, Minnesota 55199

Mary Clare O'Brian
188 Jackson St.
Littleburg, Wisconsin 53538

July, 1967

Dear Mary Clare,

Just a quick note to let you know that I will be in Milwaukee August 2–4. I would love to meet you if your parents are able to get you to the Pfister Hotel in downtown Milwaukee.

I only have one possibility to meet with you on the afternoon of August 3. If you are able to make it, I could meet you in the main lobby at 1:00 p.m. Please drop me a line to let me know one way or another.

Fondly,
Mother Monica

16

Mary Clare brushed her hair one hundred times, watching as it swelled and frizzed in the bureau mirror. She swore her hair got curlier every day. While Kelly and Jen and Sandy all wore their hair straight with a little flip at the end and had bangs that curved perfectly at their eyebrows, hers lay in tight little curls. She had tried for a long time to offer her wretched hair up to Jesus, but right now she wasn't doing any sacrifices.

As far as she was concerned God had not kept his end of the bargain with the miracle of riches she had expected. She still talked to God, but she kept it to a minimum, curt, like the way her parents talked to one another when they were done fighting but still mad. Making her work like this—God just didn't seem fair.

She hadn't, however, given up the idea of becoming a Mother Superior. For one thing, she could end up stuck dealing with her humiliating hair forever if she didn't cover it up with a veil. She liked the special privileges that came with running the household, which, she thought, was a lot like being Mother Superior. She not only controlled the younger kids but had gained the respect of her older brothers—at least where meals were concerned—and she also got special privileges from her parents, as long as her requests didn't require "time off." If she wanted to make popcorn at midnight, it wasn't a problem. If she wanted to have a friend spend the night, it wasn't a problem. So maybe her parents would even be willing to give her a little bit of money.

The thought prompted Mary Clare to drop her brush on the dresser and dash to her closet, where she pulled down her box of saints and glow-in-the-dark statues. There she had tucked a newspaper ad that could save her pride and her hair. It was for a new product—Curl Free—a permanent that took curls out of a person's hair. But it was really expensive, almost five dollars. She wondered if her parents could even come up with the money if they wanted to. And what would happen if something went wrong.

The very idea of having straight hair made Mary Clare stroll down the stairs with more confidence and determination than usual. She wore her baby-doll pajamas and held the Curl Free ad boldly in her hand.

As she approached the kitchen she heard the back door open and the clicking of high heels in the doorway. Mom was home. She glanced at the clock: 10:30 p.m. Now that it was getting closer to the opening of Mom's play the practices were getting longer and more frequent, and since Mom had the lead she always had to be there. Mom dropped her books on the table and grabbed a glass from the cupboard, which she filled with water and drank down before she said a word.

"Just a few more weeks of this," Mom said. Mary Clare wasn't sure whom her mother was trying to reassure.

"You seem exhausted," Mary Clare said.

Mom nodded. "I am. But it's a good kind of exhausted. I'm having a wonderful time."

Mary Clare held out the ad and her mother took it.

"You're kidding. A permanent to *straighten* hair? What will they think of next?"

Dad joined them in the kitchen, carrying a beer. A little clump of hair stood up on top of his head where he had been twisting it again. He did this automatically when he was lost in thought.

"What are you talking about?" he asked.

Mary Clare looked down at the floor. It was awkward for her to talk to her father about personal things.

Mom handed him the ad. When he read it he laughed and smiled broadly at Mary Clare. "I like your hair curly," he said. He twirled his hair. "Do you really want this?" he asked.

Mary Clare nodded.

"We'll just have to find the money for it," he said.

Mary Clare jumped up and gave her father a hug.

"With all you've been doing around here, you deserve it." He gave Mom a critical look that suggested she didn't do much at all.

It seemed to Mary Clare that her dad was slowly getting used to her mother being back in school and the plan for her to teach in the fall. He was still finding fault with the new way things were done. He'd get mad if he didn't have more than a couple of pressed and starched shirts to choose from in the mornings, and though Mom found rides three days a week to and from school, he had to give up the car on the other two days and work out of the house. And Mary Clare suspected that his pride was wounded when he discovered that he didn't have the power to forbid Mom from doing something she really wanted to do. But at least they were talking again. Mary Clare prayed that he was adjusting to Mom's decision.

The back door swung open again, revealing the unusual sight of Matthew, Mark, and Luke together.

"What's going on?" Luke asked.

"Well, if it isn't the Three Musketeers," Dad said. "I hope you boys are staying out of trouble."

The boys mumbled that they were. Matthew pulled a jar of peanut butter out of the cupboard.

"We're out of bread," Mary Clare said.

"Crap," Matthew said. He perused the refrigerator to see if there was something he wanted to eat.

"I just remembered something," Dad said. "Mark, you got a letter from Flipper today. Let me get that for you." He returned to his office and came back a minute later with the envelope. He handed it to Mark. "It's actually addressed to the whole family, but I wanted you to open it."

"Is he almost done with basic training?" Mary Clare asked.

"Yeah," Mark said. "Three more weeks." He opened the envelope and pulled out a single sheet of paper with writing on both sides.

Dear Mark and O'Brian family,

Whoa! This place is something else. Parts of it are great, like getting in shape, but parts of it aren't so great. Mrs. O'Brian, I'd kill for some of your lasagna. I miss all the lively table discussions, especially when Mr. O'Brian is home and gets into one of his stories.

The other part that stinks is when I look at my battalion and realize that some guys will return home missing arms or legs, and some won't come home at all. I can't help thinking of that when the number of soldiers being killed rises daily.

Anyway, it will sure be worth it when I get out of here. I'll get my GED and let Uncle Sam pay for college.

Mary Clare, thanks for those cookies. I gorged myself before I shared any with the guys.

See you guys as soon as I get my leave.

Love,
Flipper

P.S. Holy moley, Mark, we thought some of the teachers at Littleburg High were strict. Try marching in the rain for five hours because one guy didn't make his bed right!

Flipper in the army.

Mary Clare tried to imagine his shoulder-length blond hair shorn off into a crew cut. She tried to picture him in army fatigues but couldn't.

Dad broke the silence. "It sure brings back memories. I remember marching in boot camp until guys dropped. But the discipline helped. None of us could have withstood the conditions of war without it." He looked at Matthew. "And the war made a man out of me."

Matthew swallowed a bite of the cold macaroni and cheese he had discovered in the refrigerator. He dropped his fork. "Fighting the government is no picnic either. I'm finding my own way to become a man," he said.

Dad scowled and shook his head. "Any word from Selective Services about your appeal?" he asked.

"No," Matthew said. He raised his chin and looked defiantly at Dad, "But I'm sure that I'll win."

"Flipper sounded pretty cheerful," Mark said, clearly trying to change the subject.

"That was really nice of you to send him cookies, Mary Clare," Luke added.

Mary Clare nodded. At the moment, she was more concerned about removing the Curl Free ad from the table before her brothers saw it and started making fun of her. She leaned against the table, reached back, acting as if she were straightening her shirt, and crumpled the ad in her left hand.

"G'night," she said, slipping backward toward the stairs.

"Wait a minute," Dad said.

Mary Clare swung back around, praying he wouldn't say anything about her hair.

"Your mother mentioned that you wanted to meet a mother superior in Milwaukee on Thursday. I can take you."

Mary Clare stood frozen at the kitchen door.

"You're kidding, a mother superior?" Luke asked.

"I knew she was going to end up a nun," Mark said. "I never have to pray because I figure she prays enough for all of us."

All three boys laughed at that.

"C'mon," Matthew said, "leave her alone."

"Paul, you shouldn't have said anything in front of the boys," Mom was saying, but Mary Clare was already running up the stairs to her room. She sat on the edge of her bed, too upset to lie down. Hot tears streamed down her cheeks. Mary Clare had kept her correspondence with Mother Superior a secret.

17

The heat was sweltering in what Dad called "the dog days of summer," and it was only the first day of August. But Mary Clare was going to walk the mile to the pharmacy anyway. She had to. Not only did she finally have the money to buy herself the Curl Free permanent, but she had a fistful of invitations to her party to drop into the mailbox in front of the store. She had even filled in a few extra invitations without names. She carried these in her pocket in case she ran into someone she had forgotten. Besides, she wanted to look good when she met Sister Monica the day after tomorrow.

Dad was home today, so she could get away to the store without dragging the little kids along. And Joannie was going with her. She often came over when Mary Clare was knee-deep in laundry and housework. They'd get talking and Joannie would simply pitch in. Mary Clare had also invited Kelly to meet them at the drugstore, and Kelly had actually said yes. It would only be the third time she'd seen Kelly this summer. But Mary Clare missed her old friend. She secretly hoped that if Kelly got to know Joannie, she'd like her and they could all be friends. Besides, she was really nervous about the perm and felt she could use both girls to help her with it. She had made them both vow to keep the perm top secret in case something went wrong.

"Who would I tell?" Joannie had asked. "You're the only person I hang around with." Mary Clare had given her a quick hug of appreciation.

Now Joannie joined her on the walk to the pharmacy. They started out down the hill, ignoring the heat and walking at a strong pace. But by the time they turned onto Madison Avenue they were so hot they had slowed way down.

"I wish I'd brought enough money to get a Coke," Mary Clare said. "I just sweated out every bit of liquid in me." She looked at Joannie, who was still dry and fresh looking, and rolled her eyes.

"I can't help it," Joannie said. "I just don't sweat."

"Well, if I ran into any guys," Mary Clare said, "I'd absolutely die."

When they finally reached the pharmacy Mary Clare was relieved not to see any familiar faces at the soda counter. She and Joannie searched the aisles themselves after Mary Clare told a clerk they didn't need any help.

Then Mary Clare saw it. The box lay under an orange "on sale" sign at the tail end of the hair product aisle. Mary Clare held it like a prize in her hands. The box featured two pictures: a "before" picture, in which a girl with horrible hair just like Mary Clare's was looking mortified, and an "after" picture, in which the same girl's perfectly straight hair framed a radiant smile.

Mary Clare and Joannie were reading the back of the box intently when they were interrupted.

"Hello, girls." It was Sister Charlotte holding a small bag.

Mary Clare swung around, knocking three more Curl Free boxes off the shelf. Sister immediately bent down to help the girls pick up the fallen products. As soon as she read the label Sister laughed, a hearty laugh that wrinkled her nose and showed off her dimples.

Mary Clare felt herself tense defensively, but she relaxed when she saw that Sister Charlotte was not laughing *at* her. Sister wasn't like Mark and Luke.

"If I'm not mistaken this is for you, Mary Clare," Sister said, running her hand lightly over Mary Clare's curls. "I'll definitely have to see the end result."

"Oh, you will!" Mary Clare blurted.

Sister nodded, but Mary Clare saw a brief change in her face—a flash of something—sadness maybe—in her eyes. It was there for a split second, then disappeared. She wondered what had made Sister react like that.

"Mary Clare's having a party with a band and everything," Joannie said.

"You are!" Sister said.

"Yes, Sister. You *have* to come to my party," Mary Clare said. "I'm having my brother's group play and everybody in the whole class is invited, even all the boys." Mary Clare handed her one of the extra invitations. "Mom said it would be okay to have boys since we're going into seventh grade and the party will be chaperoned."

"I know. Your mother asked me my opinion, and I told her I thought it would be fine," Sister said as she opened and read the invitation. "Oh," she paused. "We don't usually ..." She paused again, but steeled herself. "I'd love to come to your party. I'll do my best to be there. It would be wonderful to see you kids—how you've all grown over the summer. Thank you, Mary Clare."

"You're welcome, Sister," Mary Clare said. She was dying to ask Sister if she knew her mother would be teaching at Maria Goretti in the fall. She also wanted to ask Sister which of the lay teachers was leaving and who Mom was replacing, but she couldn't ask. She had kept Mom's confidence and hadn't said a word to anyone. Instead, Mary Clare peered at the little brown paper bag Sister was holding. She tried to imagine what a nun would need from a drugstore.

Sister shifted the bag from her right hand to her left uncomfortably. She seemed to know what Mary Clare was thinking.

"Well, girls, I've got to get back to work," Sister said.

"What work?" Mary Clare asked. She knew immediately that the question was rude and could feel the heat rush to her face. But she'd often wondered what the Sisters did when they weren't teaching. How else could she imagine her eventual life as a nun?

Sister flashed a knowing smile. "Nuns have to do housework like everyone else, girls." She held up the bag. "We even need things like toothpaste and shampoo. This afternoon I'm doing several loads of laundry and then cooking dinner."

"Oh," Mary Clare said. "Well, good-bye Sister."

"Bye Sister," Joannie said.

Sister waved a quick good-bye and left the store.

Since the Curl Free was on sale, Mary Clare had just enough money to get chocolate Cokes for herself, Joannie, and Kelly, who arrived just as they were about to sit down at the counter. While Joannie and Mary Clare drank the refreshing drinks greedily, Kelly took tiny sips and seemed ill at ease about something. But neither Mary Clare nor Joannie could get her to admit what was going on.

By the time they were halfway up the Jackson Street hill, all three girls grappled with the heat in silence. When they reached Becky's house, Mary Clare could make out her own. She noticed several kids sitting on the porch stairs. At first she assumed they were friends of Gabby or Anne, but as they drew closer she recognized Jen, Sandy, and Tina. They were all waving.

Mary Clare turned to see Kelly shrugging her shoulders, her face scrunched and eyes watery. Joannie looked puzzled.

"What's going on?" Mary Clare asked.

"I didn't mean to, but I did it. I told Jen. About your hair, I mean. It just slipped out." Kelly said.

Mary Clare couldn't think of anything to say. She hurried past Kelly, her heart racing. They'd been best friends since second grade and Kelly had never, ever broken a confidence before.

Kelly raced in front of Mary Clare and stopped, facing her. Mary Clare stopped, too, but only because she was out of breath. She looked past Kelly to the girls waiting on the porch. Had they knocked on the door? She hoped nobody in her family was fighting. She hoped her dad was in a good mood and wouldn't embarrass her.

"Wait!" Kelly said. She turned Mary Clare's face toward hers. "I'm really, really sorry. I knew they'd be excited. I wanted you to be part of the group again. If you want me to go home I will."

For a split second Mary Clare considered telling her to go, but then she melted into a smile. "C'mon, let's give me the greatest hair in Littleburg. It looks like we have a lot of help."

"Hey," Sandy said when they reached the front porch. "Are you gonna let us watch?"

"We couldn't let you do something this big without us," Jen said.

"Let me see if my dad's okay with you all coming in."

"I don't think anyone is home," Jen said.

"Yeah, we knocked and rang the bell but nobody answered." Sandy said.

They were right. When Mary Clare looked for her father and the kids, she found a note on the kitchen table instead.

Mary Clare,

Went to Janesville to run some errands. Have all the kids with me. See you around dinnertime. Have fun with your uncurling project and be careful.

Dad

Mary Clare let out a yelp. She couldn't remember another time in her life when she'd had the whole place to herself. She read the note to her friends.

"It's a party," Joannie yelled. Kelly helped Joannie select some singles they could play on the living room record player while Mary Clare pulled out the Curl Free directions. She and Joannie read them together, gave each other a look of surprise, then read them again.

"It's so easy!" Joannie said.

"I know, I thought it would be like a complicated math problem," Mary Clare said.

The strong smell of ammonia had both girls holding their noses while trying to mix the two solutions together in the plastic bottle. Mary Clare placed the pointed top on the bottle and slipped into the plastic smock that was included to protect her clothes. Kelly ran to the bathroom for towels. Everybody was making noises about the bad smell, so Jen and Sandy opened the windows to air out the room.

The perm only included one pair of gloves, so the girls took turns squirting the stinky solution into Mary Clare's hair and combing it through. When her hair was saturated, Sandy set the timer.

"Is it normal for it to sting my scalp this badly?" Mary Clare asked.

The friends all looked at each other. None of them had experience with permanents except Joannie, whose mother gave her a regular perm last summer.

"It doesn't say anything about it on the box," Joannie said.

"You only have to keep it on for sixteen more minutes," Sandy said.

"Sixteen minutes is a long time when your head's on fire," Mary Clare said.

"Just think how cool you'll look," Kelly said.

"We'll all have to teach you how to manage straight hair," Joannie said.

"Is it really bad?" Sandy asked.

"No," Mary Clare lied.

"You have to suffer to be beautiful, you know," Sandy said, her perfect flip bouncing as she shrugged her shoulders.

Mary Clare opened her mouth to say that whoever started that saying should be shot, but the phone rang and she got up to answer it instead. She motioned to Joannie to turn the music down, but apparently Joannie didn't hear because The Supremes continued to sing out so loudly that Mary Clare had to ask who was calling three times before she could make out the words from the other end of the line.

"Mother Monica?" Mary Clare asked, stunned. She could hear the needle scratch the record on the phonograph and then the music stopped.

"Yes, am I speaking with Mary Clare?"

The voice sounded very professional.

"Yes. It's Mary Clare. I didn't expect ... I'm just so surprised you called."

"Yes," Mother Monica said. "I *had* to, really. I suppose you know by now that we're going to have to cancel our appointment in Milwaukee."

"No, I didn't know. I didn't know anything about you canceling our appointment." Mary Clare looked up to see that her friends had made a circle around her. They were all listening intently. Now they would all find out that she planned on becoming a nun. Well, they couldn't be too surprised.

"I thought that by now you'd have heard about the Negro uprising in Milwaukee. It's all over the news. The National Guard's been called in and the city's on complete curfew. We can't have a conference in that environment." She sounded irritated.

"No, Mother Monica, I didn't know anything about it."

"We're hoping to reschedule as soon as we can travel safely. I don't think Milwaukee residents are feeling good about Religious right now."

"Oh," Mary Clare said. She wasn't sure what the situation in Milwaukee had to do with Religious.

"I hope it won't be too much trouble for you and your parents. I would enjoy meeting you."

"Me too," Mary Clare said.

"I'll call you as soon as we have a date," she added.

"Thank you, Reverend Mother," Mary Clare said.

When she hung up, she could see that her friends had a million questions. But Mary Clare couldn't stand the burning on her scalp for another second. "Wait!" she screamed. She ran to the sink and started rinsing.

"You've still got ten minutes," Joannie said.

"You're probably wrecking it," Jen said.

Kelly leaned over the sink to help Mary Clare rinse. "Oh, your poor head," she said.

The tepid water was the only thing that stopped the burning. Mary Clare rinsed for a long time. Then she lifted her head out of the sink and accepted the towel someone handed her. She patted her hair gently, not wanting to rub against the raw scalp.

Joannie handed her the mirror she'd retrieved from Mary Clare's room.

When Mary Clare took one look at herself in the mirror, her painful scalp was forgotten. She was looking at perfectly straight hair. *Thank you God!*

Her hair was wet, of course, but there wasn't even a hint of curl. Her friends took turns combing it and watching it dry in the sweltering heat. Mary Clare felt pampered. She felt beautiful.

When her friends asked her about the call from Mother Superior, Mary Clare admitted she was considering the convent. But she made light of it. "Meeting her will give me good material for my diocesan essay addendum," she said. "I thought it might give me an edge."

"Great idea," Kelly said.

"You'll win that fifty bucks," Joannie said.

Mary Clare heard the telltale thump of the afternoon newspaper hitting the front door. She scrambled to the door to find out what the paper had to say about the riots in Milwaukee.

There it was, the headline of the *Daily Jefferson County Union*:

MILWAUKEE NEGROES ON RAMPAGE

Mary Clare switched on the television. She had to wait for the commercial on Lux soap to end before the 5:00 news started on NBC. One by one her friends joined her in the living room to see the clips of National Guardsmen wearing helmets and driving jeeps down desolate Milwaukee streets. The footage showed the aftermath of the angry mobs from the previous night: broken glass from store windows, shattered windshields, debris in the streets, fires here and there.

"It looks like we've just been invaded by the Communists or something," Tina said.

"It sure doesn't look like this is our country," Sandy said.

"To think it's only an hour and a half away," Joannie said.

"The Negroes did this to their own neighborhood," Jen said.

Mary Clare leaned forward to hear the announcer.

"There remains speculation that this violence is related to the civil rights activism of Father James Groppi, a white Catholic priest who serves as the youth advisor for the local NAACP chapter," the newscaster was saying.

Mary Clare had heard of Father Groppi before. Everybody had. He had marched with Martin Luther King in Selma, Alabama. But now she wanted to know more about him.

18

●●●

Mary Clare preened and pampered herself over the next several days, enjoying her glorious hair and how it flipped perfectly at the ends with just a little bit of coaxing. She had been afraid to rest her head on the pillow those first few nights for fear that her glorious hair would wind its way into curls while she was sleeping. The first night she had awakened several times to look at her glorious hair in the hand mirror she kept under her pillow. But when, after several nights, her glorious hair had remained gloriously perfect, she had relaxed and allowed herself to fall into a deep sleep.

But tonight was different. Tonight brought with it the anxiety of tomorrow. She would wash her hair for the first time since the perm, knowing there was a chance it would surrender to the water and shampoo and curl up. Tomorrow brought with it the trip to Milwaukee she both dreaded and looked forward to. Dreaded because she didn't know what Mother Superior would be like in person. Looked forward to because of the excitement of going to the place where Father Groppi was brave enough to lead the march for civil rights.

Mary Clare remembered how Mother Superior sounded on the phone. That tone in her voice. At first she had reasoned that the Reverend Mother was just irritated because she'd had to change the date she was going to Milwaukee, but she'd made that comment about Religious probably not being very popular in Milwaukee at the moment. Now that Mary Clare had been keeping up with the news, she realized that Mother Superior had been talking about Father Groppi. She hoped that Mother Superior was talking about how other people felt. Surely she didn't blame Father Groppi for the riots. He was a man of peace.

Mary Clare yawned. She was tired, but the idea that Mother Superior might disapprove of Father Groppi made her wonder. If she wasn't going to be the Mother Superior right away, she'd have to be obedient to the Mother Superior. Could she really be obedient to someone who didn't approve of fighting for what you believed in? Did she really want to give up boys? Her thoughts flashed to Flipper. He'd winked at Mary Clare the other night at dinner while he was home on leave, and Mary Clare had melted into her chair. She'd had a warm glow ever since and wondered if he could ever like her.

And anyway, now that her hair was straight she felt practically pretty. Maybe she didn't need to keep it covered with a veil.

She yawned again and knew that she needed to say her prayers before she got too sleepy. She said a quick prayer for her family, another for her meeting with Mother Monica, three Our Father's for the civil rights movement, and a whole Rosary for the outcome of her hair. She was almost asleep when she remembered to pray for Matthew to get his conscientious objector approval.

The next morning Mary Clare stepped into the shower with the same courage and trepidation she imagined Saint Joan of Arc had felt when facing the enemy. She prayed for straight hair the whole time she washed it. But by the time she emerged from the shower, she knew she was in trouble. She couldn't see her hair at first because of the fog on the mirror, but she could feel it curling and frizzing the minute she patted it with a towel. As it dried, it got worse.

"Whoa, check out the afro," Luke said when she walked into the kitchen. It was early morning and Luke, Mom, and Dad were the only ones at the kitchen table.

"Have a heart," Dad said to Luke when he caught a glimpse of Mary Clare.

"Oh no," Mom said. "Come here and let me help you."

Mary Clare squatted in front of her mother and let her finger the mess of hair. She held back tears, but just barely.

By the time Mary Clare and her father left for Milwaukee, she felt a little better. Mom had combed through her hair using Dippity-do so that her hair was a little flatter and a bit less curly. She hoped the headband would help keep it in place.

She was dressed in a pink sleeveless shift that had to be let down so it fell just above her knees. Her shoes were the same old Sunday shoes she always wore, and since Mom insisted on it, she carried a small white purse that held a pair of white gloves. Mom had tried to make her wear a pillbox hat but Mary Clare refused. At least the headband kept the curls off her face. A hat would just draw attention to her hair.

Mary Clare's stomach felt funny when she got into the car alone with her father. She wasn't used to conversing with him about much beyond what they were having for dinner, or which one of the kids she had nursed for a cut or a bruise. She knew almost nothing about his business world, and he certainly knew little about her world. Now, she figured, she'd have to think of something to talk to him about for an hour and a half.

It turned out not to be a problem. Dad turned the radio on even before they got out of the driveway.

"I hope you don't mind if we listen to the speech Archbishop Cousins is going to give. It should be on all the main radio stations in a few minutes," Dad said. He flipped through several stations until he found what he was looking for.

"I read about that," Mary Clare said. "He's going to talk about the racial riots in Milwaukee!"

Dad gave Mary Clare a startled look. "I had no idea you were following that story," he said. Mary Clare kept a straight face but inside she smiled. It was good to see her father surprised. Now maybe he'd realize that boys weren't the only ones interested in politics. Now maybe he'd realize that she was growing up.

A broadcaster was talking about the upcoming speech. "There are seven hundred thousand Catholics in the Milwaukee area, and Archbishop Cousins has his hands full with this address. Many Milwaukeeans feel that Negroes wouldn't be pushing so hard for fair housing without Father Groppi's involvement in the NAACP, and that Milwaukee wouldn't have had a riot without him. Father Groppi's involvement in the civil rights movement has resulted in hoards of letters requesting Father's resignation and even excommunication from the church. Archbishop Cousins is expected to address prejudice and take a stand on the role of Catholic Religious in protests."

Dad shook his head. "Archbishop Cousins is totally behind the civil rights movement," he said. "But I don't know what he's going to say after all the senseless violence."

"But Father Groppi isn't responsible for the riot. He only wants peaceful protests to help Negroes get their rights."

Dad furrowed his brow and looked at Mary Clare as if she were a stranger. It was fun surprising him with information he didn't expect her to know. So she kept right on going.

"He cares about them getting fair housing and jobs. They live in the oldest and most run-down part of Milwaukee, and did you know that the police force has only eighteen black cops out of hundreds?"

"That's true," Dad said. "But try to see it from the perspective of the Polish people in Milwaukee. They've worked hard for many years to build a community. They made sacrifices to be able to build beautiful, elaborate churches. They're afraid of losing everything to the Negroes. To them, Father Groppi is a rabble-rouser." He sighed. "The Catholic Church has stayed neutral about civil rights. Now Father Groppi is forcing the Church to take a stand."

Mary Clare focused her eyes on the glove compartment, not wanting to look at her father. Did his sympathy for the Milwaukee South-siders mean he was against Father Groppi and the Negroes he was trying to help?

She continued to avert her eyes but drew up courage to ask a question. "What do you want the Archbishop to do?"

"Oh, I hope, and I pray, that he'll stand up for Father Groppi. I hope and I pray that he'll tell us that it is the duty of Catholics to pursue justice — not by rioting, but by peaceful demonstrations."

Mary Clare felt a swell of pride in her father. Something new and fragile was taking shape in her relationship with him. A union of minds. A kinship she hadn't felt until now.

"The Archbishop's speech is about to begin," the broadcaster said.

Mary Clare turned up the volume.

In a soft-spoken voice, Archbishop Cousins began:

"We have known the horrors and fears and anxieties of something that many believed 'couldn't happen here.' Unfortunately, it happened. And we must face the inevitable fact. I grieve with the victims. I extend sincerest sympathy to the families of officers and others who died or were injured in the performance of their duty to uphold law and order, without which justice is impossible."

Mary Clare looked at her father. She could see that he was

barely breathing as he listened. Archbishop Cousins continued by praising the public officials for their quick response and the news media for preventing the spread of rumors that might have incensed more violence.

"Wanton destruction, arson, potential murder can never be condoned. They are offenses against the law of God and the law we rely upon to protect us all. Yet through them we have been dramatically made aware of conditions we might have ignored, or problems we might have continued to disregard."

He spoke of the confusion in the Church regarding their role, and reminded listeners that Pope John XXIII and Pope VI encouraged everyone to work together to eradicate discrimination and injustice.

Mary Clare and her father exchanged smiles. Mary Clare stretched her arms over the dashboard to relax a little and watched a colt tromp behind its mother in the field they were passing. When she tuned back in she heard ". . . Permit me to say that it is the sacred duty of the faithful, the priests, and the Religious of our time and of our Archdiocese to root out of their hearts and to free their communities of any prejudice that would make men anti-Jewish, anti-Negro, anti-Mexican or anti- anything else that would render them anti-Christian in practice."

Mary Clare tuned in and out of the long speech without meaning to. Her mind just wandered to the upcoming meeting, and her hair, and other important things. But she was tuned in when he made his verdict on priests and nuns being involved in protests.

"From all this it follows that all Catholics, priests, sisters, and laity must take an active and intelligent part in the promotion of Christ's teachings in the field of belief, in social doctrine, in relieving poverty. We are all part of the apostolic mission of the Church. We should not be surprised then to find priests and

Religious joining with our lay brothers and sisters in espousing equal rights for all."

Mary Clare let out a cheer that was matched by that of her father. In the rest of the speech Archbishop Cousins didn't mention Father Groppi by name, but he firmly supported the nuns and priests who protested for justice. She watched her father's head nod in agreement. He swallowed hard a few times, which brought Mary Clare to tears. She wished she could protest with them.

When the speech ended Dad switched off the radio. In the silence that followed, Mary Clare couldn't stop thinking about Father Groppi and the other nuns and priests who were fighting for equal education opportunities and fair housing and other civil rights. She thought about the civil rights workers who had lost their lives in Alabama trying to help the Negros get voting rights.

"Dad," Mary Clare said, "do you think that civil rights workers are saints?"

"Whew!" Dad's whistle was piercing. He thought for a moment, then nodded. "Yes, I do," he said. "They're putting their lives in danger for what they know is right—for what they believe in their hearts is God's will. Yes, I do think they're saints."

Both remained silent for a while. Mary Clare couldn't help but think about Matthew. His was a different kind of fight. Though she knew she was getting into dangerous territory, she had to say something to her father. Had to, if she were going to be brave like Father Groppi. Finally she summoned the courage. "You know, Dad, conscientious objectors and all the protesters are fighting for what they believe God wants, too—to end an unjust war, to stop the killing."

Dad didn't say a word. But he removed his hand from the steering wheel and cupped his chin, as if stroking an imaginary beard.

As they approached the city that was still in a state of national emergency, that still had a nighttime curfew and National Guardsmen everywhere, Mary Clare had visions of the shooting, looting, and fires of one week earlier. She prayed for peace in Milwaukee. She prayed that Mother Superior would like her enough to ask her to apply to Saint Mary Magdalene Convent, even though she might not choose to go. She ran a hand through her hair and prayed that the Dippity-do would hold it down.

Once in the city, National Guardsmen and police were everywhere in their uniforms and helmets. Most of the people on the street were white, but Mary Clare counted ten black people over the next several blocks. It was the most Negroes she had ever seen in one day. Most were men but when Mary Clare and Dad stopped at a red light a black woman about her mother's age crossed the street. She was wearing a flowered miniskirt and pink blouse. She clutched a shopping bag against her thigh and gave a nervous smile to Mary Clare and her father as she walked past them.

Mary Clare leaned forward, smiling too broadly, too enthusiastically for the circumstances. The woman averted her eyes and darted to the other side of the street, leaving Mary Clare feeling small, foolish, deflated. She couldn't make up for all the prejudiced people by smiling.

"Have you noticed that some of the police are wearing black helmets instead of white?" Dad asked, motioning with his head to a policeman standing on the corner.

Mary Clare noticed and nodded.

"I heard that on the first night of the riots, the police put on their white riot helmets and quickly realized that they were sitting ducks. So a few of them raced into a hardware store, picked up black spray paint, and started painting as many helmets as they could."

Mary Clare nodded again, too overwhelmed by the subdued tension that filled the atmosphere. All these people, black and white, trying to go about their business as usual with such a strong undercurrent of anger and fear.

"Don't be nervous," Dad said.

Mary Clare realized that she'd been fiddling with her purse, opening and closing it. Taking out the gloves and putting them back in again.

"There hasn't been violence for days, and with the National Guard here there won't be. Besides, we're going to the Pfister Hotel, the ritziest in town. We'll be fine." He shook his head and sighed. "I don't know how those nuns can afford such opulence."

When they arrived at the hotel, a Negro man in a fancy uniform took Dad's car keys. Mary Clare's eyes grew wide.

"It's okay," Dad laughed. "He's the valet. He'll park the car for us and bring it back when we're ready to leave." Mary Clare slipped into her mother's white gloves and found that she was trembling as she followed her father into the fancy hotel. She told herself that with all the really important things happening in the world it was silly to be so nervous about meeting a mother superior. But it didn't work. She used to quake in front of Sister Agony, and a mother superior was a much higher authority.

Dad placed a protective arm on Mary Clare's shoulder, then stopped her just inside the lobby, where he leaned down and almost whispered in her ear. "After I meet the Mother Superior," he said, "I plan to give you two some privacy. But I'll stick close by, so don't be nervous."

Mary Clare smiled her thanks. She took in the huge lobby with its ornate chandeliers, grand wooden staircases, and Victorian furniture. There were fireplaces and several sitting areas with Queen Anne chairs, like the one her dad had picked up from an estate sale. But there was nothing tattered about these chairs. The seats were velvety and maroon.

Dad nudged her. Mary Clare looked up to discover a white-clad nun approaching her. It had to be Mother Monica.

19

● ● ●

I recognized you by your curly hair," Mother Monica said, smiling.

Mary Clare automatically reached up to flatten the mound of hair that was ever-growing in this humidity. She wanted to run but smiled faintly instead. "I recognized *you* by your habit."

Mother Monica and Dad seemed to think her remark was funny, so Mary Clare joined them in laughter.

Mother Monica was different from what Mary Clare had pictured. She was taller, older, thinner. She had a square jaw and bold brown eyes that looked Mary Clare over sharply. When Mother Monica extended a firm hand to shake Mary Clare's, her handshake was solid. Mary Clare tried to match the shake, but her palm was damp and her hand still trembled. She was disgusted with herself.

"We can meet over there." Mother Monica ushered them toward an area in the lobby that contained a settee, a Queen Anne chair, and one overstuffed green chair. She helped herself to the Queen Anne chair, looking like royalty herself with her perfect posture and authoritative face.

"Please don't think that this"—she motioned to the chandelier and beautiful furnishings everywhere—"represents how we live, Mary Clare. Our stay here was paid for by a donation from a generous man who loves this hotel." Mother Monica turned to Mary Clare's father, who had taken the easy chair next to her, leaving the little velvet settee for Mary Clare and her purse.

"Several convents in our order are meeting here tonight and tomorrow to look at possible changes in our habits," Mother Monica said to Dad.

Dad smiled. "Are you ready for such a change?"

"Not at all," Mother Superior said. "I'm quite fond of our habits. But as Mary Clare would say, I'm old-fashioned. The younger nuns find them cumbersome for the work we do, caring for infants and cooking." She sighed. "Tending our gardens while wearing white is no small feat either."

Mary Clare looked at Mother's long billowy sleeves. She couldn't imagine weeding in a habit.

"The nuns who do the laundry and iron every day find the habits especially annoying."

Mary Clare hid her shock. The image of nuns filling baskets with vegetables from the garden had seemed quaint somehow. But nuns doing laundry and ironing? She had thought that by becoming a nun she'd escape mundane household chores. She'd pictured herself doing important things like counseling the young mothers to save their souls and choosing good families for the babies. She certainly didn't want to join a convent to do more housework. And she'd have no choice. When she was a lowly postulant and novice, and for all the years it took her to become mother superior, Mother Monica could assign her any chore she saw fit.

Dad shook his head. "It's hard to keep up with all the changes," he said. "It's a new world." He moved to the end of his seat. "Reverend Mother," he said, "I'll excuse myself so that you two can get to know each other better." He nodded to a table across the lobby. "I'll be right over there."

He stood.

Mother Monica stood.

Mary Clare didn't know if she should stand or sit. She remained seated and gave her father a nervous wave good-bye.

Mother Monica patted the empty chair next to her. "Sit closer," she said.

Mary Clare obeyed. But her mind went blank. She couldn't think of anything to say.

Mother Monica offered her a warm smile. "How was your trip from Littleburg?"

"Fine, thank you." Mary Clare's voice squeaked.

"Were you nervous about the racial tension?"

"Sort of," Mary Clare admitted. But when she thought of the Bishop's speech her anxiety was replaced with excitement. "We listened to Archbishop Cousins on the radio, and he was *wonderful*."

Mother Monica nodded soberly. "I saw it on television," she said, and sighed.

Mary Clare waited for Mother to say more about the speech, but she was looking over Mary Clare, distracted by something in the lobby. Mary Clare turned in time to see two young nuns hurrying toward them. They seemed lit up with excitement, especially the fair-skinned one with the rosy cheeks. The other nun—a Negro—seemed more contained.

"We're very sorry to disturb you, Reverend Mother," the rosy-cheeked one said.

"Yes, very sorry," the Negro nun said. It had never occurred to Mary Clare that there might be Negro nuns.

"Mary Clare, this is Sister Grace," Mother Superior said, nodding toward the rosy-cheeked one. "And this is Sister Miriam."

The nuns extended their hands and Mary Clare shook them.

"We'll talk over there," Mother Monica said, nodding toward a Victorian-style table and chairs next to one of the fireplaces. The nuns waved to Mary Clare and followed her.

"Go ahead," Mother Monica said. Mary Clare could hear without even trying to be nosey.

"We have an incredible opportunity, Reverend Mother," Sister Grace said. "Father Groppi is going to lead a march today from St. Boniface to the safety building—a police station and jail—and several of us would like to join them."

"No," Mother Monica said, barely waiting for Sister Grace to complete her sentence. "I cannot permit it."

Mary Clare was so shocked she forgot to pretend she wasn't listening. She looked at the two disappointed nuns and at Mother Monica's stern face. The Mother Superior towered over the two young nuns. Her chin jutted out as if she was offended by their request. Sister Grace looked down at her feet, but Sister Miriam didn't flinch. "It would mean a great deal to me, Reverend Mother," she said. "They're protesting unfair housing. All my life I've wanted—I want to help make a difference."

"I understand, Sister Miriam," Mother Monica said in a cool voice that didn't really sound understanding. "But I will not put you or any of my Sisters in harm's way."

Sister Grace opened her mouth to say something but Mother Monica raised a hand, demanding silence. "And I won't contribute to the image of the Religious as radicals who stir up trouble. Surely that is not why you became nuns."

During the long silence that followed, Mary Clare could barely stay seated. She picked at a loose thread on one of the arms of her chair. Anger consumed her. She wanted to jump up and argue that the nuns wouldn't be in any more danger than Father Groppi and the brave protesters who had the courage to stand up for equality. She wanted to tell Mother Monica that Religious should fight for justice, and taking a stand only looked bad to people who didn't care about justice. This was the same Mother Superior who'd been kind to her—told her not to worry so much about sins, sympathized when Mom was pregnant and when she lost the baby. Now she seemed so cold.

"Reverend Mother, I believe that protesting wrongs is serving God," Sister Miriam said.

"That's possible," Mother Monica said, "but Mary Magdalene Convent won't participate. We serve God through the work we do with unwed mothers and their babies."

"Reverend Mother," Sister Miriam said.

Mary Clare would have loved to hear what she had to say but Mother Monica stopped the conversation cold. "Thank you, Sisters," she said. That was all. That was the final word.

Mary Clare could hear the rustling of their habits as the two nuns walked away. She peeked up at them and found their faces to be as desolate as she felt.

When Mother Monica returned to her chair, she looked pale and exhausted, as if the brief conversation she'd had with the Sisters had drained her of every ounce of energy. Yet she managed a smile for Mary Clare.

Mary Clare could not return the smile. She looked from Mother Superior's face to the purse she was holding on her lap, hoping to hide her anger. But Mother Monica knew.

"So, you heard my conversation with the Sisters," she said.

"I didn't mean to," Mary Clare said.

"Of course you did," Mother Monica said. "You want to know all there is to know about being a nun—and especially about being a mother superior. Besides, we weren't all that far away."

Mary Clare could hear the smile in Mother Monica's voice. She nodded reluctantly.

"And you didn't like what I had to say."

"I don't understand," Mary Clare said carefully. But when she saw that Mother Monica expected her to say more, a dam burst inside of her. "How can you say no to the nuns when the protest is so important? How can you think that the nuns and priests protesting for justice make the Church look bad? I think it shows that the Church cares about all people. Religious like Father Groppi and Archbishop Cousins help Catholics see that we have a responsibility to do the right thing. Your sisters just wanted to help with an important cause. You called it rabble-rousing, but I think it's just helping people wake up."

"The role of the Church is to bring people to God, not to fight the government, Mary Clare." Her words were slow and patient.

"Are you sure?" Mary Clare didn't even pause to consider that she was talking to a mother superior. "Father Groppi and Archbishop Cousins think it's important for Religious to take a stand. What I don't understand is why would God tell you one thing and tell Father Groppi and Archbishop Cousins something else?" Mary Clare was shaking again.

Mother Monica didn't respond. She looked even more exhausted than before.

Something caught in Mary Clare's throat and she couldn't go on. She let out a breath she didn't know she had been holding, and with it came tears she didn't even try to control. *Mother Monica should know the answer*, she thought. *With her position in the Church she should be able to hear God clearly. When she tells the nuns what to do, it should come right from God.* But judging from Mother Monica's face, it was clear that mother superiors didn't know everything.

"Do you think there is only one way, one truth, one answer?" Mother Monica asked.

"Of course," Mary Clare said. It was a silly question. "And one

God," she added. But she remembered then what Becky Turner's mom had said when she tried to convert Becky to Catholicism because it was the true religion. "Everybody thinks they have the true religion," she had said. She bit the inside of her mouth and felt her shoulders slouch involuntarily. Everything was so confusing.

"One God, of course," Mother Monica said. "But what if there are many answers, many truths that all exist together like different colors of the same rainbow? All I can do, Mary Clare, is pray, and listen to my heart for what God wants."

Mary Clare liked the image—all those beautiful colors, reflecting from the same source but all beautiful and all moving in the same direction.

Mary Clare sat. Mother Monica sat. It seemed that neither of them could think of anything to say.

After a while something occurred to Mary Clare and she couldn't stop herself from saying it out loud. "You don't hear God any clearer than other people, do you?" She hadn't meant it to sound like an accusation, but it did.

"I don't know. I don't know how other people hear God. I hear by listening to my heart."

Mary Clare felt the fire of her convictions flare inside her once again. "But if I listen to my heart I come up with different answers."

"Yes, I know. If you were Mother Superior, you would have told the Sisters to march, and you would have marched right with them."

Silence.

"And what would you have done if you were a Sister under me, and I told you not to protest?"

Mary Clare held her eye contact with Mother Monica. "I would have done everything I could to change your mind."

Mother's eyes were smiling but she held her chin firm. "Yes, you would, wouldn't you?" Her voice softened. "And if you didn't succeed in changing my mind?"

Mary Clare lowered her eyes. She held her jaw tight to prevent the truth from slipping out, the truth that both of them knew. The truth that Mary Clare could not take a vow of obedience. The truth that knowing this, Mother Monica would never accept her into St. Mary Magdalene Convent. Mary Clare hugged herself against the hurt. She had failed, failed, failed.

Suddenly Mother Monica laughed. "My dear," she said. "If you were in my convent I'm afraid you'd spend half your time doing penance for your strong will and spunkiness."

Mary Clare didn't think this was funny. She wished that she could be obedient. She wished that she could believe that Mother Monica knew God's will for her and simply follow that will without questioning, thinking, searching for truth on her own. It would be so much easier to have someone guide and take care of her.

"Then you'd probably quit on me and—who knows?—start your own convent."

Mary Clare lifted her head and leaned forward. This was something she had thought of before. "Like Saint Clare," she said. "She started her own convent with the help of St. Francis."

Mother Monica's eyes widened as she saw that Mary Clare had taken her seriously. "Or you could just do wonderful things as a layperson," Mother Monica said, quickly recovering from her shock. "You could have a career or become a wife and mother."

"Or both," Mary Clare said.

Mother Monica raised herself from the chair and beckoned for Mary Clare to do the same. Mary Clare allowed herself to be wrapped in the embrace Mother offered. She was aware of the same Ivory soap smell as Sister Charlotte, but Mother Monica's scent was mixed with something else, something musky—like incense. Mary Clare wanted to stay in that embrace forever. She felt safe. Mother Monica was mother. She was Mother Church.

"Whatever you do with your life, Mary Clare, you will do it well. You will do it with passion and love. I will continue to pray for you every day, and I hope you will pray for me."

For a second Mary Clare wondered why a Mother Superior would need prayers, but then she remembered that Mother was really just a human being.

"Thank you," Mary Clare murmured. "I will."

Dad must have seen them get up because the next thing she knew he was standing next to them.

"You have a wonderful daughter," Mother Monica told Dad.

"I think so too, Reverend Mother," he said, shaking her hand good-bye.

This time Mary Clare started the hug with Mother.

"I hope you'll continue to write," Mother Monica said.

Mary Clare nodded. But even before she stepped into the car that the valet brought around, Mary Clare knew she was finished writing letters.

"Can we go past the protesters?" she asked Dad once they were a few blocks from the hotel.

"It's too dangerous, Mary Clare. And it would delay us for hours."

But they did end up getting a clear view of the protest. Dad had to go several blocks out of his way because of road construction, which landed them on a street where they could clearly see the protesters crossing the 16th Street viaduct. The protesters were singing a hymn Mary Clare didn't know and carrying signs that said "Fair Housing Now!" and "Black is Beautiful."

Mary Clare opened the window, leaning out to wave and

yelled "Hooray Father Groppi!" before her father had a chance to reach over and stop her. But when he saw that a few of the protesters were waving back, he waved too. They didn't see Father Groppi, but Mary Clare spotted several nuns and priests in the crowd. She even spotted two nuns in the white Good Shepherd habits and wondered if they might be Sister Miriam and Sister Grace.

20

Mary Clare placed the phone back on the receiver and put a check next to Pat Flanagan's name to show that he was coming to the party tonight. Practically everyone was coming. Of the forty-six people who had RSVP'd, only three kids weren't able to make it.

When she heard the mailbox lid clamping shut she said a quick prayer for Matthew and ran to pick up the mail. She had gone through this ritual for three weeks. Each day she would search the mail for an official-looking letter for Matthew and would brace herself for Matthew's call, only to tell him it hadn't come.

But today, the day of her party, she was more anxious about the mail than usual. If Matthew got his letter and the news was good, he'd be in great form for playing that night. But if the news was bad, he'd be devastated. He'd be making plans, once again, to defect to Canada. Maybe if the letter came today she should try to read through the envelope, or steam it open. Maybe if it came today she should hide it somewhere until after the party.

Mary Clare made the sign of the cross before she pulled out the thick pile of mail. She sat on the top porch step to look through it. She sorted mail into the usual three stacks: bills, stuff from Dad's company, miscellaneous. On the rare occasion when anyone else got a letter or magazine, she would make a fourth pile. Today she was almost to the end of the stack when she saw Matthew's name. She glanced at the return address. It was the letter. She frantically gathered the piles of mail and headed inside. Having the letter Matthew had waited so long for right here in her hands, Mary Clare knew that she couldn't hide it or open it. She had to do the right thing. She had to call Matthew right away. When she set the letter on the kitchen table and was about to reach for the phone, another envelope, one she hadn't realized was there, slipped to the floor. It had been hidden under the envelope for Matthew. Mary Clare reached down and picked it up. This one was for Matthew too, and it was also from the United States Government.

Mary Clare glanced at the clock as she dialed Matthew at the apartment he was sharing with a friend in Madison this summer. It was 4:00 p.m. He should be here by 6:00 with the rest of the band to set up. *Please be home, please be home, please be home,* she whispered. But no one answered. She counted twenty-seven rings before placing the phone back on the receiver. She would have to wait.

The sound of the back door slamming startled her. Matthew's voice followed. "Hey little sister, doing any civil disobedience lately?"

"No!" Mary Clare said, too loudly. "But you got some mail." She sounded almost hysterical. She held out the two letters.

Matthew froze. "There's two letters," he said, without reaching for them.

When he finally took them from her, he studied them carefully without looking inside. Suddenly he began to laugh. A hard, angry laugh. He looked at Mary Clare, who hadn't moved away from the phone. "One of these is a draft notice," he said in a thin voice.

Mary Clare nodded.

He looked back down at the letters. "One of these is a draft notice but it's the other one that's going to change my life, because the other one will tell me if I've won the appeal or not." She nodded again.

"Actually my life will change either way," Matthew said. "It's a matter of which direction it will take."

"Open them," Mary Clare said.

Matthew set the envelopes on the table. "The house sure looks nice," he said, noticing the freshly mopped floor and the clean kitchen counters. "I guess you're ready for the party tonight." He walked over to the refrigerator. "Do we have anything to drink?"

"Open the letters," Mary Clare said.

The way Matthew abandoned the refrigerator and fell into a chair at the kitchen table made him look like a Raggedy Andy doll. All the strength seemed to have drained out of his body.

Mary Clare pulled a pitcher of lemonade from the refrigerator and poured him a glass. She sat down beside him. Matthew's face was gray, his eyes dull. He took a sip of the lemonade.

"I can't," he said, and slid the letters toward Mary Clare. He buried his head in his arms on the table. "You read them for me."

Mary Clare carefully ripped open the first envelope. It was the draft notice. She held her breath as she read the words. "It says you are to report for duty on Monday, October 2, 1967."

Matthew didn't move.

Please God, please, please, please. I'll do anything, she prayed as she reached for the second envelope. She paused, thinking about how hard this summer had been because of her bargain to be a saint, and how God hadn't kept up his end of the bargain by giving them the money she'd expected. She quickly modified her prayer. *Not anything, Lord — I'm no saint — but I'll certainly try to be a good person if you let Matthew get to be a conscientious objector.*

Mary Clare tore the envelope open and scanned the words.

Dear Matthew O'Brian,
We are pleased to inform you . . .

She squealed and Matthew's head popped up. He grabbed the letter from her hands.

"Oh, thank you, God!" he said. "This is so cool. Thank you, God." He danced around the kitchen. "That priest I told you about from the seminary — Father Duane, he wrote a letter for me. It must have made the difference." He picked the letter back up and studied it. "I'll be hearing about my conscientious objector work in a few weeks," he said.

"What work do you think the government will have you do?" Mary Clare asked.

"I have no idea, little sister, but it won't be killing people." His voice was thin, but the color had returned to his face. He set the letters side by side on the table. He shook his head. "And to think my draft notice and deferment came on the same day."

He leaned over Mary Clare and smacked a kiss on her forehead. "Thanks for all your prayers," he said. He tousled her impossible hair.

Mary Clare smiled as she followed Matthew's pacing with her eyes. He paced the kitchen, then wandered into the living room and dining room and paced them too.

"Where is everybody?" he hollered. "Where are Mom and Dad? I want to spread the good news!"

"Dad's on his way home from Chicago — he could be here

any minute—and Mom's at the store picking up a few last-minute party things. Gabriella and Anne have sleepovers at friends' houses. And the little kids are having an overnight at Gallagher's farm."

"Okay," Matthew said. He reached for the phone.

"Mom and I made seventeen pizzas."

"Okay," Matthew said with a dismissive wave. "I gotta make some calls."

Mary Clare took a last critical look around the main floor. Everything seemed to be in as good a shape as possible, and now she had to get herself ready. She ran up the stairs to take a shower. As she undressed, she thanked God over and over for Matthew's good news. But Mary Clare also remembered what she'd told God before she'd opened the envelope. She had started to bargain with God, to say that she would do *anything* if God let Matthew get conscientious objector status. But she had suddenly been overcome with weariness. Now she tried to explain her reaction to God and to herself. *I'll never be demure and sweet and obedient like the Virgin Mary. I don't want to turn the other cheek like Saint Theresa. The best I can do, God, is be a regular person who tries to do good things.*

When Kelly and Joannie arrived early Mary Clare was taken off guard. She'd forgotten that she'd asked them to help her straighten her hair. But at the last minute she reconsidered. She looked at her wet hair in the mirror, knowing full well that as it dried it would also curl and as it curled it would shrink until it was half its current length. But it was okay. Her hair was natural. Not like everybody else's.

"I'm going to leave it like it is," she said.

Kelly and Joannie were shocked. "Do you want to wear a headband, at least?" Joannie asked.

"Should we slick it down with Dippity-do?" Kelly asked.

"No," Mary Clare said. "It's fine." She ignored the looks Kelly and Joannie were exchanging and headed downstairs. They followed.

21

● ● ●

The party seemed to take off by itself. One minute there were Kelly, Joannie, Mary Clare, and a fledgling band warming up, and the next minute the driveway and backyard were swarming with kids sipping lemonade and chatting in little groups of four or five. The Seminarians were set up partway in the garage "for acoustics," Matthew said, so the driveway filled up with kids first, then spread out into the backyard as the party swelled to fifty or sixty people by the end of the first hour.

Mary Clare was suddenly blinded by someone who had come up from behind and covered her eyes. The hands were too rough and big to be Gregory's. Besides, she'd been keeping track of Gregory and he was on the opposite end of the yard with all the other guys.

"Guess who?"

The voice sounded strange, but when Mary Clare caught a whiff of Wrigley's spearmint gum she knew. She pulled the hands away from her face and spun around.

"Flipper!" she squealed. He was dressed in full army uniform, including an army hat on his perfectly shaved head. She couldn't help looking shocked at his baldness. But Flipper just laughed and grabbed her in a spontaneous hug. A hug! From a soldier! In front of all these people! Shivers of delight shot through her body. "It's so great to see you," she said.

"I wanted to make sure I had a chance to see all you guys, and Mark thought it would be okay for me to crash your party," Flipper said.

Mark was standing behind him, but Mary Clare hadn't noticed him until right then. He was smiling, happy to be with his best friend.

"How long are you home?" she asked Flipper.

"Just 'til Monday, then I leave for Nam."

"Wow! That's really short," Mary Clare said.

"That's what I keep thinking," Flipper said, taking in the wide circle of friends that had gathered around them. Mary Clare could see by their wide eyes that they were impressed by Flipper's uniform.

"If it's okay with you, I'd like to stick around for a while, hear Matthew's band, and talk to your folks."

"Sure," Mary Clare said. "Mom's in the kitchen getting food ready and Dad's right up there." She pointed to the top step on the back porch where he had perched himself. She could see his foot tapping to the band's version of "Barbara Ann." "Ba, Ba, Ba, Ba, Barbara Ann ... Ba, Ba, Ba, Ba, Barbara Ann ..." His lips moved along with the song.

Everyone seemed mesmerized by the Seminarians. Her friends were amazed at how many songs they knew and how well they played them. They could even play some of the brand-new songs.

"I heard it through the grapevine," everyone sang along with the band. Joannie leaned into Mary Clare's ear, "I just got the single for this. These guys are good."

208

"This is the coolest party," Sandy said. "I think I have a crush on Carl. Watch how his hair falls over his eyes while he's looking down at his guitar."

"I've been watching Butch," Jen said. "His smile is gorgeous."

Matthew was at the microphone, "We wanna see you guys dance out there! Let's get this party moving."

"Play 'Twist and Shout,'" yelled a kid Mary Clare didn't even recognize. She studied the crowd. There were lots more people than she invited. It seemed like her party was the biggest thing in Littleburg.

In a minute the popular Beatles song rang out and several of the girls started to do the twist. By the end of the dance almost everybody was dancing.

Mary Clare looked through the crowd until she found Gregory, who was half talking to a few of the guys and half watching her. She waved, trying to look casual. She didn't know what to do except ignore him. If she approached him, he might ask her to dance and she'd be self-conscious. If he didn't ask her to dance, she'd have to ask him to dance, and he might say no. Better just to stay away.

She noticed that one of the potato chip bowls and two pizza pans on the picnic table were empty. Mary Clare figured that her mother was probably tied up in the kitchen, so she swooped them up to refill them herself. But when she got inside the kitchen, her mother wasn't there. The oven timer showed three more minutes, so she knew more pizzas were coming up and Mom would probably be right back. So she pulled another two bags of chips from the pantry and started filling the bowl.

Soft secret-sharing voices echoed from the living room. Then she heard a giggle that could be no one but Sister Charlotte. She crept to the kitchen doorway and listened in. She'd confess the sin of sneaking at her next confession, but she had to listen.

"But I wasn't going to let that … that woman stop me. Believe it or not, I climbed out my bedroom window and walked over here."

The peel of laughter came from her mother. "Good for you. I don't know how I'm going to stand her as my principal."

Mary Clare stood frozen—except for her mouth, which dropped open as she realized that they were talking about Sister Agony. She had never heard an adult talk about a Religious that way—and one of those adults was Sister Charlotte.

"God be with you!" Sister Charlotte said.

When the timer went off, Mary Clare knew she had to make a quick escape. She couldn't face the party, or Sister Charlotte, so she bolted into the downstairs bathroom, almost knocking her mother down in the doorway. She plunked herself down on the edge of the bathtub. She had to sort out what she had just heard and what it meant.

Sister Agony must have said no when Sister Charlotte asked to go to the party, and Sister Charlotte snuck out anyway. Why would Sister Charlotte disobey her superior? She had taken a vow of obedience. Sister Agony was mean, everyone knew that. But Sister Charlotte had never shown anything but respect for her.

Suddenly pieces started fitting together, creating a picture Mary Clare didn't want to see. Mary Clare remembered how Sister Agony flaunted her power over Sister Charlotte when they received the diocesan essay contest letter. She had opened Sister Charlotte's mail and read it to the class. She had practically scoffed at Sister Charlotte's new habit. She remembered that flash of sadness in Sister Charlotte's eyes that day in the pharmacy when she said it would be good to see everyone in the class again. What was the big deal? She'd see everybody in a few weeks anyway, unless …

Unless it wasn't Mrs. Simmons leaving. "A teacher from one

of the older classes is leaving," Mom had said. Mary Clare had assumed it was Mrs. Simmons, of course, because she taught eighth grade and had just gotten married, and most married women didn't work.

It was Sister Charlotte who was leaving. The shock of it felt like concrete settling inside her stomach. Sister Charlotte must have requested a transfer to a different school.

Mary Clare hated Sister Agony for being so difficult. But Sister Charlotte broke one of the vows she'd made to God. And why? Just to come to a party? It didn't make sense. Mary Clare could understand if Sister broke her vow to do something important like protest the war in Vietnam or march for civil rights, but a party? Unless Sister Charlotte wasn't transferring at all. Unless she was leaving the convent altogether.

Mary Clare had to know. If Sister Charlotte was leaving the convent, this might be the last time Mary Clare would see her. She wouldn't tell anyone else, but she had to talk to Sister Charlotte. She pulled herself up from the side of the bathtub, wiping hot tears from her eyes. She steeled herself before returning to the party.

On the way out the door, Mary Clare passed her mom in the kitchen.

"I'm making another triple batch of pizza dough," she said, smiling. Mary Clare gave her mother a quick peck on the cheek.

"Thank you so much," she said. "The food's wonderful."

"Thank God I bought a whole case of tomato sauce and way more toppings than I thought we'd need," she said. "I suspected we'd end up with half the town."

In spite of her heavy heart, Mary Clare felt blessed. Nobody else's mother made homemade pizzas for their parties. Nobody else had a brother in a band.

Outside the party was hopping. The boys and girls were no

longer separated in the least bit. Everybody was dancing with everybody. Mary Clare had to smile. This was exactly the way she pictured it, laughing, dancing, singing, eating. Dad had even put torches up in the yard so that there was enough light, but not too much. The ambiance was perfect.

"There you are," Gregory said, coming up behind her. He frowned. "I haven't seen you dance once."

"So you're keeping track," Mary Clare said lightly. "I haven't seen you dance either."

The band started to play another Beatles favorite, "If I Fell in Love with You." Gregory smiled mischievously. "I bet you're chicken to slow dance with me."

"No," Mary Clare said automatically. She didn't know if she meant "no" she wasn't chicken or "no" she wouldn't dance with him. It didn't matter. Gregory took her hand and they were dancing before she could say anything else. Mary Clare was stiff at first, but then she relaxed.

"Did you finish your addendum?" Gregory whispered in her ear.

Mary Clare shook her head. "Not one word of it."

"I did," he said, "and I'm sorry to tell you that it's sure to be the big winner." His eyes sparkled as he said it.

"You are soooo conceited," Mary Clare whispered. She'd never been so close to a boy's ear before.

Gregory grinned.

For a minute Mary Clare was self-conscious about being a head taller than Gregory, but the thrill of dancing—slow dancing no less—with a boy won out, and she lost herself in the moment.

When the band took a break a few minutes later, Mary Clare could see Sister Charlotte making her way to the house. She wriggled her way through the crowd to catch up.

"I have to talk to you, Sister," Mary Clare said when she caught up with her.

"Of course!" Sister said. She looked at Mary Clare expectantly.

"Privately," Mary Clare said.

Sister followed Mary Clare through the house and up the staircase to Mary Clare's room. Mary Clare switched on the light and closed the door behind them.

Sister's wrinkly nose smile turned into a look of concern as she took in Mary Clare's serious expression. "Aren't you enjoying your party, dear?"

Mary Clare nodded.

"I know you've had way more than your share of responsibility this summer. Your mom was thrilled to be able to do this to thank you."

Mary Clare nodded again. "Sister," she said abruptly. "I know that you're leaving."

Sister Charlotte sat down on the bed. Her face looked stricken. "Did your mother . . ."

"No," Mary Clare interrupted. "I figured it out." Tears flooded her eyes again and she felt violently ill. Sister wasn't denying it, so it had to be real.

"I have to know, Sister. I have to know if you're leaving Maria Goretti or leaving the convent."

Sister bit her bottom lip and lowered her eyes. Even in the half-darkness of the room Mary Clare could see that Sister's face had turned pale.

"I can't discuss this, Mary Clare. I'm not allowed to."

"Please, Sister. I'm sorry to be nosey, but I'm trying to understand so many things. Things about being a nun and vows and how convents are changing and . . . and everything. You're the coolest nun I've ever known and if you're leaving . . ."

Sister let out a long sigh. "I'm sorry to let you down, Mary

Clare. I am leaving the convent. I haven't even been allowed to speak to the other nuns about this, but I'm leaving in the morning."

"Sister, why?"

"I can't give you a simple answer to that. It's complicated. The Church is changing, the convent is changing, but none of it is changing as fast as I am."

"Then it's not because of Sister Ago—Sister Agnes?" Mary Clare asked.

"You mean Sister Agony?" Sister Charlotte laughed, and Mary Clare couldn't hide her shocked expression. "I know you kids call her that, and, unfortunately, so does she." She let out a sigh. "No. Sister Agnes is difficult, and she represents much of what I don't like in the traditional Church. But I'm leaving so that I can be myself and serve God in other ways."

"I was going to become a nun," Mary Clare blurted.

"I know," Sister Charlotte smiled tentatively. "Are you still thinking about it?"

"No," Mary Clare heard herself say. And, for the first time she knew it was true.

22

It's for you again," Anne said, stretching the phone cord across the kitchen to reach Mary Clare at the sink.

Since the party a week earlier, kids had been calling in a steady stream to say thank you or to ask when The Seminarians were going to practice again. And now everybody knew about Sister Charlotte leaving since Father Dwyer announced it at Mass last Sunday. He hadn't said that she was leaving the convent, of course. Just that her time had ended at Saint Maria Goretti parish. And Mary Clare had kept Sister's confidence as the kids all hugged each other and cried in the vestibule of the church after Mass. She'd also remained silent about her mother replacing Sister.

"I can't say anything either," Mom had said. "It's Father Dwyer's place to make the announcement."

Typically the end of August meant long days and nights in the kitchen canning bushels of tomatoes and cooking and freezing corn they'd buy from local farmers. But this year Mom was determined to stock up on freezer-friendly meals. "That way we can thaw something out in the morning and we'll just stick it in the oven when we all come home after school," she had assured Mary Clare.

Mary Clare had never seen her mother so excited and energetic. In preparation for working full-time, Mom's attention and energy were completely on the family right now. Her attention on the family felt like the sun was beaming throughout the home, making everybody shine through. Right now she had everybody working in a flurry of activity. Anne's job was to gather all the uniforms to see which fit one of the girls and which required mending or alterations. Gabby and Martha were cleaning out their drawers and the older boys were in charge of cleaning out the garage. Mom wanted everything ship-shape before school started again.

Mary Clare sighed. She wanted her mother to be this happy doing housework every single day, but she knew better. What made her mother shine today was the knowledge that she would be doing something more than housework and childcare tomorrow. What made her brighten the family today was the realization that in a week she'd have a career as a teacher. Housework, cooking, changing diapers, and wiping noses would only be a part of her life from now on.

This was why so many of Mom and Dad's friends were turning against her. They all knew she'd be working soon. They just didn't know she'd be taking Sister Charlotte's place. Even Mary Clare's friends said hurtful things, pretending that they were simply repeating what their parents had said.

"My mom thinks that women are supposed to stay at home and take care of their kids," Kelly had said when they were walking home from the park. "It's how God wants it."

"My dad said he'd never tolerate a wife who worked. He said you kids will be neglected," Joannie said.

Mary Clare had wanted to lash out at them and say mean things back about their parents. Instead she bit her lip to avoid committing another sin and ran ahead towards the stream that cut through the park. She had squatted and stared into the water, pretending to look for fish and frogs and unusual stones. But the words of her friends still stung. Maybe they were right. Maybe Mom was a bad mother. Maybe she was being cheated having to work so hard.

"Don't just stand there, Mary Clare, hop to," Mom said now. "You can wash this pan and use it to start the water boiling for the pasta."

Mary Clare stopped remembering and accepted the dirty kettle her mother held in front of her. She couldn't help smiling when she broke out in song while browning the hamburger on the stove.

"How are things in Glaca Mora? Is the little brook still sleeping there?" Mom sang.

Mary Clare remembered the song from the musical *Brigadoon* that the community theatre had put on last year. By the second verse Mary Clare couldn't help joining in.

She knew that Kelly and Joannie were probably long done with their measly chores—picking up their rooms and taking out the garbage. They were probably free right now to have fun. But she couldn't help wondering if they ever had this kind of special time with their own moms.

On Sunday Mary Clare dreaded going to Mass. Surely Father would have to make the announcement today that Mom would be taking Sister Charlotte's place. And when he did people were going to react. Some people might support her, but it would surely be controversial. Mary Clare thought her mother was brave. She just wasn't sure that she was as brave as her mother.

Sure enough, Father Dwyer made the announcement right after the final blessing.

"As you know, Sister Charlotte's departure left a position to fill at St. Maria Goretti School. When classes begin on

September four, Mrs. Paul O'Brian will join our staff as the sixth grade teacher." There were a few gasps. "She will replace Sister Charlotte." Many more gasps followed. Father raised a hand, signaling silence. "We want to extend a warm welcome to Mrs. O'Brian."

Mary Clare could feel shock waves ripple through the church. There were whispers behind her but she couldn't make out the words. Her mother sat stiff and stared straight ahead.

She glanced down the pew. Every family member was present today. Mom had returned to Sunday Masses just after she lost the baby. Dad bent his head and continued mouthing the words to the rosary he held, as if he'd heard none of Father's words. Mary Clare knew he had heard everything.

In the vestibule, Mom smiled as people congratulated her. Several commented on how amazing it was that she could hold a job outside the home with so many children. The bite in their words was so close to the surface of their sweetness that it stung right through. Others walked right by without saying a word. Mary Clare heard one woman ask if anyone knew what parish Sister Charlotte would be teaching in. Mary Clare was grateful for the assumption that she had merely been transferred.

"What I can't understand," Mary Clare heard Mr. Carney say to his wife, "is why Father is replacing a nun with a lay teacher."

"I know," Mrs. Carney said. "Why not just get another nun?"

Mary Clare caught Matthew rolling his eyes. He bent down and whispered to her, "People don't realize that nuns are leaving the convent in droves."

"That wasn't so bad," Mom said when they were all in the car and on the way out of the parking lot.

"I guess not," Dad said. "But I think a lot of people are wondering why I can't support my family myself."

"No, they don't," Mom said. "I'm just glad it's over with. In a few weeks everyone will have adjusted and it will all be fine."

"I won't adjust," Gabby said. She hated the idea of having her mother at her school.

"I'll adjust," Anne said, poking Gabby in the side.

"Me too," Martha said.

"Me three," Margaret said.

That made Dad smile.

Part 3
Fall

23

On the first day of seventh grade, Mary Clare watched more than listened to Sister Georgette, their new teacher. She and Sister Agony were the last of the nuns to wear the old habit. Sister Georgette was stocky, with a big red nose that she nursed constantly. A long white handkerchief would magically appear from her sleeve, and then she'd use it on her nose and return it. Yuck. When Sister Georgette was nervous, which was often, her entire face turned red to match her nose. Students called her "Sister Sniffles" behind her back. Mary Clare hoped that Sister had been spared knowing about this insult. She couldn't imagine going through a whole year with someone as blah as Sister Georgette, especially remembering how Sister Charlotte had lit up the classroom.

The shrill sound of the intercom interrupted Mary Clare's thoughts. Sister Agony began her litany of messages:

"Welcome to a new school year at Saint Maria Goretti School. It is a privilege to receive a Catholic education. First and second graders, remember to wait for the crossing guard to help you across Main Street. Seventh grade Camp Fire Girls will have their first meeting after school tomorrow in the cafeteria. Remember that all book fees are due in this office by Friday,

September eight. Finally, will Mary Clare O'Brian and Gregory Kowalski please report to my office after school."

Gregory motioned to her, holding a manila folder with the words "Diocesan Essay" printed on the tab. Mary Clare sighed. She hadn't done the addendum. She had thought about it a thousand times over the summer, but something she couldn't quite put her finger on stopped her each time. Now it was due.

Gregory waited for her at the door. "I'll show you mine if you show me yours," he teased.

Mary Clare shrugged.

"You're kidding!" Gregory said. "Ten bucks. Ten bucks is the least you can get for just writing the addendum—we're finalists!"

"I'll get it done before the deadline," Mary Clare said.

She repeated the same words to Sister Agony after Gregory's essay had been accepted with a smile.

Sister Agony puffed up in her chair. "You had all summer, Mary Clare. Now you have less than *two weeks*." She hit the desk with her hand for emphasis. "I want to see one of you two win this contest," Sister Agony said. "In fact, I want one of you to win first place and the other second. It would benefit the school."

Gregory leaned in toward Sister Agnes. Mary Clare could see the anger in his eyes. "You mean the money?"

"No," Sister said, a sour look on her face as if the mere idea were distasteful. "It shows that Saint Maria Goretti School is producing top-notch students." Sister turned her attention to Mary Clare. "Of course, I did think that if you won the money you could help your parents by putting it toward your tuition. Your poor mother has to teach full-time just to make ends meet."

Mary Clare was shaking with rage. It took every ounce of strength to keep from lunging at the nun. She took a deep breath instead, stood with as much dignity as she could muster, and looked the nun straight in the eye.

"My mother *wants* to teach. She *wants* a career. And the money she earns from teaching means that I don't have to help with tuition." She walked out tall, her chin up high. Gregory was right behind her.

"You're dismissed," Sister Agony called after them.

Gregory snickered. *I'll write the addendum,* Mary Clare thought, *but it won't be about winning. It will say exactly what I want to say.*

24

When Mary Clare hadn't turned in her addendum by the following Wednesday, even her mother started cranking up the pressure. It seemed unfair that Sister Agony had daily access to her mother. It seemed unfair to her mother too.

"It's hard enough having that negative woman telling me that none of my teaching ideas will work. Now she's badgering me because you're not getting your work done."

Mary Clare was helping Mom make a salad to go with the chicken casserole in the oven. Anne could be heard clanking silverware against glasses and plates as she set the table for dinner. Luke's voice rang through the house as he practiced a new song on his guitar.

"Don't worry, Mom," Mary Clare said. "I'll do it right after dinner." She pulled a tomato off the windowsill and washed it for the salad.

"You're darned right you will. But this is so unlike you, Mary Clare. What's the problem?"

Mary Clare didn't respond. She wasn't quite sure what the problem was, except that each time she'd pulled out paper and pencil with the full intention of writing, she'd get jumpy inside and do something else instead.

A loud thud drew Mary Clare's attention. She turned to see Mark looking like he'd seen a ghost. He dropped his books on the kitchen table. "You guys," he said in a barely audible voice. Mom turned her attention to him. His lips were colorless and his eyes brimmed with tears. "I got some news."

"What?" Mary Clare and Mom asked simultaneously.

Mark took forever to get the words out. He'd open his mouth, then close it again. His hands were in tight fists on top of the table as if he were ready for a fight. Finally he took in a sharp breath and the words that had been caught inside came tumbling out. "It's Flipper. It was a land mine," Mark said. His face crumpled. "He just got there, man. He *just got there.*"

Mom stood frozen holding a pair of tongs in the air. Mary Clare still held the knife she'd been using to cut tomatoes and grabbed the back of a chair with her other hand.

"No," Mary Clare said. "That's not true." Her words sounded like they were coming from someone else. Someone in a long tunnel.

Mary Clare was vaguely aware of thumping as someone, probably Anne, ran up the stairs. In a minute the guitar stopped playing and Luke raced down to them, his face a mess of emotions. Mom opened the arms that were holding Mark to let Luke inside their embrace. They were all sobbing. All except Mary Clare. She was still there in the kitchen, could still feel her back against the corner counter where she had somehow placed herself. She could hear the sobs. But she wasn't a part of it. She merely watched, hearing the words and watching her family from a distance.

The phone rang and Anne answered it. "Yes, we know," Mary Clare heard her say shakily.

Gabriella sauntered in through the back door, her cheerful expression giving way to concern as she saw everyone's faces.

More words. More tears.

Matthew, Mary Clare thought. *I have to tell Matthew.* She knew he was resting in a makeshift bedroom in the basement. Her arms and legs were like Jell-O but they managed to take her down the stairs. She knocked on the door.

"Stay out!"

She walked in anyway.

"Hey, you can't just ..." he started. But when he saw Mary Clare's face, he bolted upright from the bed he was lying on. "What's the matter? You look like a ghost!"

Matthew was dressed in a white uniform. White shirt, white pants—even the shoes at the side of his bed were white. His hair was pulled back in a rubber band. On his shirt pocket he wore a badge that said SAINT MARY'S HOSPITAL, MATTHEW O'BRIAN, ORDERLY. It was the job he'd been assigned for his conscientious objector service. So far he'd been working the night shift.

"Flipper," she said. "It's Flipper."

"Oh, God," Matthew whispered. "Oh, dear God."

Mary Clare wondered about God. Wasn't this all His fault? Or didn't He even care?

"Come upstairs," Mary Clare said. And Matthew followed.

●

Dinner could have been at Joannie's house. It was that quiet. Mom led the evening prayer, as she always did when Dad was gone. Tonight she added a prayer for Flipper and his family.

Even the little kids seemed to understand that something profound had happened. They were quiet, looking from Mom to each of the big kids, trying to understand. Forks shifted food around plates but very little made its way to anyone's mouth.

Finally Margaret broke the silence. "I'm glad you didn't sign up, Mark," she said. "I would cry so, so hard if you got killed." Mary Clare suspected that everyone had been thinking the same thing. Mark's face flooded with emotion—anger, sorrow, maybe guilt.

After dinner, Mom thawed a pan of lasagna to take over to Flipper's family the next day. Matthew went to work and Mark and Luke and their friends gathered in the Pad. Mary Clare could hear Mom crying on the phone when she talked to Dad. The younger kids were all playing upstairs, so Mary Clare crept into Dad's office where she could be alone with her thoughts and grief.

She sat in the rocking chair and let the tears come at last. She'd never known anyone who died before. Until now, getting killed was something she heard about on the news or read about in the paper. All of a sudden, it was here, in her life, someone she knew and cared about. Mark had said that Flipper believed that the war in Vietnam was God's will. But it couldn't be true. The idea of God willing pain and suffering for anyone made her stomach hurt.

Mary Clare regretted that she had let the addendum go so long. How could she write it now, when she was heartbroken over Flipper's death? How could she write it when she was so different from the person who wrote the first essay?

Of course. That was it. Every time she'd thought about writing the addendum she'd imagined writing it using the same voice she'd used in the original essay. But she couldn't do that. She wasn't the same person she'd been then. Winning had been the most important thing. She'd felt desperate for the money, and desperate to know that God wanted her to be a saint. She had wanted to find the right words to impress the judges. But so much had happened since then. And she didn't want the same things. She wasn't planning to become a saint or even a nun. God had answered her prayer for money in a completely different way than she had expected. Besides, she had other things she wanted to say.

Mary Clare picked up her pencil and began to write.

Mary Clare O'Brian
St. Maria Goretti Parish
September 5, 1967
DIOCESAN ESSAY ADDENDUM

You asked that this addendum go deeper into our spiritual lives. Well, that's pretty difficult because I'm changing so much. Like so many Catholics I'm confused about a lot of things. But I am also quite certain about other things.

It all used to be so simple: you tried your best to follow all the rules in the Church, went to confession, and hoped you could be good enough to get to heaven. But these days it seems like every tradition and rule has a question mark next to it. Does God really want us to worry about every little sin or do we trust that God is forgiving? Does God really want women to be subservient to men and have no power in the Church, or did the Church misunderstand? If God is love, then that means seeking justice for everyone.

There are several things that I am sure of. Things about me, things about God, and things about the Church. I am sure that I'm not the kind of girl who can be quiet and sweet, like the Church shows the Virgin Mary and St. Theresa. I am sure that Christ wants us to fight for justice like he said in the Beatitudes. And I am sure that when God gave us free will, it meant that we were also free to interpret God's Word—which is pretty scary because we have to use our brains and our hearts to figure out the truth.

I used to believe that holy people like priests and bishops and mother superiors could hear God better than the rest of us, but I don't think it works that way. I think people hear different things from God because of our own beliefs and maybe because of what we want to hear. That explains why Father Groppi and Archbishop Cousins hear God telling them to fight for civil rights while Mother Monica hears God saying that Religious shouldn't concern themselves with civil matters. It explains why some people fight in Vietnam because they believe God wants them to, and others become conscientious objectors because killing is against their beliefs.

I think the people who originally thought God wanted women to be submissive to men were men. They heard what they wanted to hear. Some people still believe that for a woman to disobey her husband is to disobey God. Not me. I think if I tried to be a docile person, I wouldn't be Mary Clare O'Brian. I'd be someone else.

It seems to me that our Church and our whole society is just beginning to wake up after a long sleep. We're waking up and wanting to make things better in our world. Maybe we're just now learning how to listen to God.

One thing I know is that God gives us gifts and he doesn't want us to bury them. He wants us to use them. I will take a vow of obedience — but not a vow to be a nun and listen to someone else tell me what God wants. My vow will be to listen to God with my own ears and my own heart. I could never be a saint like Saint Theresa or Joan of Arc, and I don't want to be a martyr like the civil rights workers who die for their cause. I just want to be an ordinary person. Just a good, ordinary person.

Author's Note

Saint Training is a novel. But that doesn't mean that it's all fiction. I drew from my own childhood experiences to write it, making it loosely autobiographical but told through the lenses of a storyteller. Most of the characters are fictional, especially Mary Clare's classmates, teachers, neighbors, Saint Mary Magdalene Convent, and Mother Monica. But there really is an order of Good Shepherd nuns, some of whom have historically worked with unwed mothers and their babies. What the reader can count on to be real are the historical events and social milieu of the era.

The year 1967 was a tumultuous time in the United States. We were embroiled in an unpopular and, many felt, unjustifiable war in Vietnam. Young men were drafted into the army by the thousands and people protested in the streets. Some draftees burned their draft cards or moved to Canada to avoid serving in a war they thought was wrong. Others who opposed the war, like Matthew, applied for CO status, which meant they could do government-assigned work instead of serving in the military.

The Civil Rights Movement was still in full force as well. The Milwaukee riots were real. Father Groppi and Archbishop Cousins were real people. Father James Groppi (1930-1985), a priest at St. Boniface parish on the north side of Milwaukee in 1967, was renowned for his zealous crusading for civil rights. His involvement with the 1965 march from Selma to Montgomery, Alabama, brought attention to the priest, but it was his tireless work against social injustices in Milwaukee that made him famous. He became an advisor for the NAACP and organized protests against segregation in Milwaukee public schools and marches for fair housing. The 16th Street viaduct in Milwaukee was considered the division between the north and south sides and was the site of daily marches in 1967. Later it was made a historical landmark and renamed the James E. Groppi Unity Bridge.

The attention Father Groppi brought to the Catholic Church placed the Archbishop of the Milwaukee diocese, Archbishop Cousins, in the difficult position of having to take a stand on the Civil Rights Movement and Religious involvement in issues of social change. He met the challenge when, in August 1967, he gave his speech *Christian Conscience and Community in Crisis,* in which he declared that it was "the sacred duty of the faithful, the priests, and the Religious of our time and of our archdiocese to root out of their hearts and to free their communities of any prejudice that would make men anti-Jewish, anti-Negro, anti-Mexican, or anti anything else that would render them anti-Christian in practice."

The Second Vatican Council, or Vatican II, was responsible for much of the confusion in the Catholic Church. Pope John XXIII had called the council of bishops to convene for spiritual renewal of the Church and to bring the Catholic Church into the modern world. The sessions began in 1962 and ended in 1965, but the effects of the council's decisions had only recently begun to show in the Church. The Mass was changed from Latin to English (or whichever language the people in the parish spoke), the liturgy changed, and laypersons were called to participate more in the Mass. The altar was turned around so that the priest faced the people. People receiving Communion no longer knelt at rails and received the wafers on their tongues, but had them placed into their open hands. Priests like Father Groppi began incorporating more contemporary music into the Mass. The Church improved its relationship with non-Christian religions and Christians of other faiths. And the council opened the door for sweeping changes in Religious orders. Like Mother Monica and Sister Charlotte, nuns began altering their habits. As convents took a good look at themselves and their traditions, many nuns chose to leave the convent altogether.

The teaching style in Catholic schools also changed. The authoritarian Baltimore Catechism, which had been a staple in Catholic schools for years, was tossed out. The idea that God is to be feared was replaced by a more accepting attitude, teaching that God was a God of love, not anger.

The women's movement in 1967 was also in its early stages. Betty Friedan's book *The Feminine Mystique* (1963) sent shockwaves throughout America while striking a deep chord in the hearts of women, giving voice to genuine concerns. My mother did return to school and work in the 1960s in spite of having many children. And like Mary Clare's mother, she had to endure the judgment of friends who felt that a woman's place was in the home.

The 1960s were not only confusing, but frightening. And the call to "question authority" had a profound effect on every kind of authority—from government and police forces to churches, physicians, and teachers. The movement forced us to take greater responsibility for our own thoughts, beliefs, and actions. Though many longed for the security of having the world interpreted for them, the overall effect of this change was greater personal power and freedom.

Acknowledgements

Many people put time, energy, love, and caring into helping me make this book a reality. Without them I would not have ventured along the arduous but immensely rewarding path of writing this book.

Thanks to my wonderful team agents, Minju Chang and Kendra Marcus, who took the risk of signing on a first-time author. They offered a comprehensive critique of my work and were available every step of the way through the publishing process.

I could not have asked for a better editor. Kathleen Kerr is warm, charming, funny, patient, and a joy to work with. She is always open to discussion and her skilled editing made a big difference in the final product.

Thanks to Cynthia Leitich Smith, my advisor at Vermont College, who skillfully helped me sink my teeth into revision and critical writing during my first semester in the MFA program. Thanks to Mary Rockcastle and the faculty at Hamline University for developing an amazing MFA program in Writing for Children and Young Adults. A special thanks to Carolyn Coman, whose work I emulate and who mentored me during my second semester at Hamline. She helped me delve deeply into character and plot.

And then there's Gary Schmidt. How can I ever express the gratitude I feel for this wonderful man who mentored me for a full year at Hamline? He's not only one of the best writers I know, but one of the best teachers. He greeted my novel with enthusiasm and offered a vision that helped me bring my idea to fruition. When I became discouraged he'd remind me, "You're the only one who can write this book Elizabeth," and I'd manage to carry on.

Thanks to my wonderful critique group Ann Bausum, Georgia Beaverson, Pam Beres, Judy Bryan, Kathleen Petrella, and Jamie Swenson for their support and honest feedback over this and other manuscripts during our seven-year odyssey (so far). You guys are the best! Thanks to my friend, travel buddy, and roommate Jodell Sadler, who sat up late during residencies, laughing and playing with ideas for this book.

A special thanks to Donald Ackerman, who took the time to share experiences as a Milwaukee police officer during the 1967 riots.

Last but not least, I want to thank my mother, Audrey Mettel Fixmer, and sisters. My mother is almost always the first person to set eyes on anything I've written. A published writer herself, she offers a critical appraisal but is always encouraging. My sisters have shared all the ups and downs throughout the whole process, and I know they'll be there for me as I write my next books.

We want to hear from you. Please send your comments about this book to us in care of zreview@zondervan.com. Thank you.

ZONDERVAN.com/
AUTHORTRACKER
follow your favorite authors